D1400292

THE

A Troubadour's Guide

COMPLETE

to Writing, Performing,

SINGER-

Recording & Business

SONGWRITER

By Jeffrey Pepper Rodgers

Backbeat
Books

San Francisco

Published by Backbeat Books
600 Harrison Street, San Francisco, CA 94107
www.backbeatbooks.com
email: books@musicplayer.com

An imprint of the Music Player Network
Publishers of *Guitar Player*, *Bass Player*, *Keyboard*, and other magazines
United Entertainment Media, Inc.
A CMP Information company

CMP
United Business Media

Distributed to the book trade in the US and Canada by
Publishers Group West, 1700 Fourth Street, Berkeley, CA 94710

Distributed to the music trade in the US and Canada by
Hal Leonard Publishing, P.O. Box 13819, Milwaukee, WI 53213

Cover and text design by Michael Cutter

Library of Congress Cataloging-in-Publication Data

Rodgers, Jeffrey Pepper, 1964–
    The complete singer-songwriter : a troubadour's guide to writing, performing,
recording & business / by Jeffrey Pepper Rodgers
        p. cm.
    Includes bibliographical references and index.
    ISBN 0-87930-769-2 (alk. paper)
    1. Popular music—Vocational guidance. 2. Music trade. I. Title.

ML3795 .R645
782.42164'023'73–dc21

                                                                    2003052225

Printed in the United States of America

03 04 05 06 07   5 4 3 2 1

CONTENTS

INTRODUCTION

One of the powerful and beautiful things about music is that it leaves you a way to express a set of emotions that has never been expressed before. Whether or not it is earth shattering or necessary even, it's just unique, and it's something the world doesn't have.

—Kelly Joe Phelps

It might come from one little moment on a CD, remixed and reimagined in your head as you walk down the street. Or from a conversation overheard in a café, or the rhythm of the windshield wipers and the summer rain. Maybe it's the way your fingers happen to fall on your instrument, suggesting a groove and then a snippet of melody. Wherever it comes from, a song idea is an extraordinary yet everyday gift, and following it through to a complete expression of words and music—and then sharing the result with others—is the most creatively exhilarating experience I know.

No wonder, then, that so many people become hooked and want to make writing and performing songs an active part of their lives. Songwriting engages so many of your faculties, from the most intuitive/creative to the most analytical/practical, and that's true whether you have professional aspirations or just want to make music in the available time around your day job. One of the great things about being a musician today is that you can participate on so many levels. Even if you're not heading out on a cross-country tour, you can audition your songs at a local bookstore or open mic—and that may actually turn out to be the first small step toward that dream tour. The major labels may not break into a bidding war for your first album, but you can find an indie label hungry for talent or just release it yourself—you can even burn your own CDs for friends and family. And no matter what kind of career you wind up having, you can keep raising the bar on your art.

This book is written for both active and aspiring singer-songwriters, amateur and pro and all points in between, as a guide and companion for the journey from idea to song to the stage and studio and beyond. The advice and perspective in these pages is informed by my 25 years of writing, performing, and recording songs and my 15 years of interviewing singer-songwriters—legends as well as hardworking underground talents—about their careers and creative processes. Pearls of advice from these conversations appear throughout this book, along with tips and insights generously shared by managers, agents, publicists, lawyers, record-company people, and others in the singer-songwriter trade.

The opening chapters talk in detail about the songwriting process, from finding ideas to editing to collaborating, but they do *not* tell you how to write a hit song (there's a whole shelf of books for sale purporting to share the "secrets" of commercial songwriting). The philosophy of songwriting here is that if you do what you love, and pursue it passionately and relentlessly, the rest will follow. And the ensuing chapters then proceed to exactly what does follow, from performing and recording to promoting your music in a crowded marketplace. More and more singer-songwriters, both well known and obscure, oversee every aspect of their music down to the last design detail of a CD tray card, so this book offers many tips for do-it-yourselfers. It is by no means a complete business and legal guide (to find one, see Resources at the back of the book and on-line at www.jeffreypepperrodgers.com), but these pages are packed with real-world advice and lessons learned the hard way.

As a singer-songwriter, you wear many hats: composer, lyricist, vocalist, instrumentalist, frontman/woman, and often manager, agent, label executive, producer, publicist—not to mention roadie. No one is born with the ability to perform all these roles well, and that's the greatest challenge of this gig as well as its greatest reward. I hope this book inspires and supports you along the way.

THE FIRST VERSE

I can't say I'm the most disciplined writer. It's probably like anyone writes a song—where you might know two chords, but every time you pick up your guitar you hum this little melody because you can't play anything else. And that's how I started: I was just trying to learn how to play the guitar, but I couldn't play any songs because I didn't know how to play, so I'd kind of make up my own tunes. I never really played along with records, and I never played with other guys because they were guys and I was far too shy to pull out my guitar and play barre chords.

—Chrissie Hynde

If you can sing a song, you can write one. Chances are, you wrote one long before you realized what you were doing. As young kids, we instinctively and effortlessly play with sounds and rhythm—riffing off of a favorite nursery rhyme, rewriting "Twinkle Twinkle," banging on pots and pans with a wooden spoon . . . When my son was a year and a half old, I was pushing him on the swing while he leaned back into the sunlight. "My . . . up in the sky," he started singing, almost in a whisper—*my* was his word for *I* or *me* at the time. "My . . . up in the sky," over and over. His one-line song was a perfect encapsulation of that moment, and the kind of thing that's available to us all if we remain open to the sounds and emotions inside and around us.

For me, kids have been a welcome reminder that songwriting doesn't have to be a high-minded or ambitious endeavor. Some songs are just meant to be sung and forgotten on a sunny afternoon. The beauty of those blue-sky songs is that they are not a product of songwriting per se. They just appear. My son was way too young to have any notion of what he was doing or why he was doing it, so the music just flowed.

The same could be said of Chrissie Hynde, sitting in her room grappling with her first guitar chords. She started writing not because she wanted to be a songwriter, but so she would have *something* to play. Never mind if her first songs were good or bad or primitive or derivative; what matters is that she found a way

Patty Larkin

into the world of songwriting. She discovered, in an entirely unintentional way, that songwriters do not belong to some exclusive club; the only requirement for entry is the desire to create and the faith that you can. When I interviewed her, she'd spent years as frontwoman for the Pretenders and penned a number of rock 'n' roll classics, so she obviously had a greater awareness of herself as an artist. But her perspective on song craft remained as practical and humble as ever. "I'm not trying to be a great songwriter or anything," she said. "I'm just trying to keep the band playing."

It sounds easy, doesn't it? To start writing songs, you just *start writing songs*. For some people and in some phases of life, it *is* that easy. But the fact is that our culture and our own conscious minds can put big roadblocks between us and the free creation of music. Those roadblocks *seem* big, anyway, until we get out of the car, walk right up to them, and find that they are like holograms. We can poke a finger into what looked like concrete, and then drive right through.

LOVE AND THEFT

It's a known fact: Amateurs borrow, but masters steal. When someone asks me where my inspiration comes from, I tell them it comes from what I hear and love, from other artists. In the past I have admired certain songwriters so much (Joni Mitchell and Rickie Lee Jones, to name two) that I had to ban them from my stereo. Everything I was working on would sound like warmed-over versions of their songs. My process is still influenced by what I hear and like, but now it's more like osmosis than conscious imitation. My mind pinpoints what is unique or special and files it away somewhere. . . . I am trying to create the feeling that someone else's songs give me when I listen to them.

—Patty Larkin

All songs are based in some fashion on the songs that came before. In writing a song, we pay tribute to music that we love, or we steer in the exact opposite direction from the music that drives us nuts. We idolize, we satirize, we copy. We fall in love with songs; we break up and wonder how we ever could have gotten into that affair. We take *everything* personally. We listen and we remember, whether we realize it or not. Melodies, grooves, tone qualities, attitudes, images—certain musical moments have something inexplicable that hooks us and doesn't let go. And when we write songs, all these stored-away moments become the tools and spare parts that shape our new creation.

When you are starting out writing songs, it's easy to lose sight of the fact that your idols forged their style from their own idols. The young Bob Dylan obsessively copied Woody Guthrie, Okie drawl and all; the Beatles started out as a cover band, and John Lennon and Paul McCartney wrote many songs pretending to be rock legends like Roy Orbison and Little Richard. But what we remember about these artists are the moments when they transcended their influences and sounded confidently and completely like themselves (thus leading to many more waves of songwriters obsessively copying *them*).

Sometimes musicians don't want to come clean about the debts they owe to their predecessors, as a matter of ego or self-promotion. Our culture worships the *new* and *original,* so artists and those who market them naturally devote a lot of energy to presenting their music as the product of some kind of immaculate conception. It's new! It's different! (But not so different that you'll think it's weird!)

You'll hear musicians talk about being "self-taught" with a tinge of pride. Well, maybe they didn't have formal lessons with a teacher, but what about all those records they wore out, the performers whose every onstage move they studied? It's OK to be perceived as having influences, but *clone* and *wannabe* and *soundalike* are the ultimate critical put-downs. And the difference between what is derivative and what is "influenced by" is very much in the eye and ear of the beholder. When the sources of inspiration are more obscure, more diverse, or more artfully disguised, the odds go up that the music will be seen as new or original.

None of this is to suggest that being original is an unworthy goal. Quite the contrary: creating something fresh and unusual brings the deepest kind of satisfaction. But keep the concept of originality in perspective. If you feel so much in the shadow of your heroes that you despair of ever seeing the light, remember that the difference between what your heroes did and what you are doing is a matter of degree. In Patty Larkin's words, it's the subtle difference between osmosis and conscious imitation. The raw material for the creative process is the same—all the songs out there floating in the ether. Everyone starts out imitating, and with time and experience we figure out how to sound less like our heroes and more like ourselves. That means lots of listening and lots of writing, and stealing *more* rather than less.

I'm accused all the time of ripping off this song or that song. Usually it wasn't something I was directly conscious of. You can never outright deny it, though, 'cause songs do have a life of their own, and who's to say what floats in and out of your head. I think copyright laws are pretty useless when it comes to songs. They're ineffable and they all influence each other, and I think that's how it's supposed to be. All our heroes listened to stuff and were influenced by it. Song is really primal, and since the very first song I think they've all bounced off each other. Like dust is still bopping around from the original big bang.

—Dan Bern

In the end, what keeps us from endlessly rehashing old songs is our human inability to make perfect copies. Our hands don't keep the beat like a metronome does—they speed up and slow down and add that mysterious but plainly audible thing called *feel*. And in writing songs, our imaginations don't just cut and paste what we hear like a computer does. Music goes into us and through us and comes out . . . different. Plagiarism happens, and even experienced songwriters catch themselves unconsciously "writing" a song by someone else. But it's a mistake to police yourself too closely and block the flow of music. And although you may occasionally need to distance yourself from your heroes (as Patty Larkin did, banning Joni Mitchell and Rickie Lee Jones from her stereo), it's also a mistake to refrain from loving and learning other people's songs out of fear of copying them. There's nothing more educational and inspirational for a songwriter than getting inside a great song and discovering what makes it tick.

Nashville musician Tim O'Brien sheds a useful light on the relationship between other people's songs and your own. He has

Tim O'Brien

seen this issue from all sides: he's had a long career as a singer-songwriter; his songs have been widely covered by country, folk, and pop artists; he's covered other people's songs onstage and on record (his collection of Bob Dylan songs, *Red on Blonde*, was nominated for a Grammy); and he's performed and recorded lots of traditional roots music. The differences between these modes of music making, he has learned, are much smaller than they appear.

> *Lately I've resolved the dilemma of my identity: i.e., am I a song-writer or a traditional musician? Really, I could spend all my time in either direction but could never decide what to concentrate on. Then I realized, sometime while working with Darrell Scott, that you can't help imitating even when you write something new, and conversely, you can't help but be a little bit different from what went before. Even if you do a rendition of an old song, you'll put something of yourself onto it.*
>
> —Tim O'Brien

For a songwriter, the revelation that you can't help but be yourself is very liberating. I always remember a comment from Peter Mulvey, a folk-rock troubadour who as a teenager fell under the spell of the legendary guitarist (and brilliant songwriter) Leo Kottke. On Mulvey's first recordings, the Kottke influence was easy to hear. But over time, it became much harder to trace, as other influences accumulated and mixed with Mulvey's own emerging musical personality.

> *When I was 19, I just wanted to be Leo Kottke. But the thing is, I don't have either the strength or the speed and never will. And also I'm not him. There's that glaring flaw, that gaping hole in the plan, that I am not, in fact, Leo Kottke.*
>
> *I think all you do as an artist is you hear things that you think are cool, and you go out and you try to do them and you fail. And that failure produces your own art—hallelujah.*
>
> —Peter Mulvey

THE MYTH OF PERFECTION

I don't think it's my job to perpetuate a myth of perfection as an artist. I really liked reading Charles Bukowski and Anaïs Nin and authors who would let me see their process, let me see how they developed. Because as a young kid, I thought, "OK, this is something I can do. You don't just start out writing The Grapes of Wrath." *And so I've never wanted to look more perfect than I am in the public eye, because why would you want to alienate people from thinking they can do what you do? I think a lot of artists enjoy that gap—they like perpetuating the myth that they are sort of a special chosen race of artistically perfect, fit people. But it's not true—there are a lot of songs I've written that aren't very good, and all you can do is put out what's honest and keep going and developing with time and just focus on development more than anything.*

—Jewel

Think of a favorite track by a singer-songwriter you love. Play the song in your head, and savor the sound and style. Beautiful, isn't it? So tightly written, so powerfully performed, so crisply recorded.

Now think about everything that made that moment possible.

For starters, there's all the writing and growth that had to occur before the artist could write that particular song. Every songwriter has to work through the pale imitations, the half-baked concepts, the nice-try experiments, the can't-figure-out-what-else rhymes, the lumbering melodies, to get to the good stuff. Every time you fall short of your mark, you gain invaluable knowledge and experience. You understand mistakes you won't make in the same way again. You imagine a different approach to try next time. In other words, any song you write, no matter how good or bad or ugly you think it is, serves a purpose beyond itself: it moves you along to the place where you can write your *next* song. Behind every songwriter's best work lies a long trail of lesser tunes that did their job and can be retired from the repertoire.

Songwriting aside, many other kinds of experience help to make that favorite track of yours shine. There are the gigs, which show musicians how their own assessments of their songs square against reality—where they discover, for example, that the song they were slightly embarrassed about is in fact a crowd pleaser and that their lofty piece of musical poetry doesn't quite get across. Every performing situation, whether a dream showcase or a gig from hell, teaches something about communication that artists can apply to their next gig. And the same is true of time spent in the studio. Each track recorded is an object lesson, and musicians constantly reassess their working methods in light of their past hits and misses.

Not only does that track you love reflect hours and years of playing experience, but it is shaped by technology. There were the bad takes you never heard, the flubbed notes that were edited out, the effects applied, and the many rounds of tweaking during the process of mixing and mastering. All these adjustments were guided not just by the musicians, but by the engineer and producer and bystanders who offered their ears and opinions—all toward the goal of hooking your attention right from the downbeat.

Finally, consider the way your track was packaged—the artwork, the notes, all the things that are, again, designed by multiple people to grab you. (If the song exists only in your collection as a digital file, well, think of a record instead.) Our perceptions of music are strongly affected by how it is presented, and we ascribe great significance to the shrink-wrap and the bar code and everything else that signifies that this is a consumer product. The goal of marketing and packaging is to present the product as fully realized, shiny and new, confident and hip. And this means sweeping under the rug the long and often messy process that made it possible.

That song you are thinking of is still a great song, and your admiration for it shouldn't be diminished by considering all the prep work that went on behind the scenes. But don't be blinded by the bright light reflecting off of that shiny disc. The disc and the sounds captured on it are just one small artifact of a long journey. And you, with your instrument and your ambitions and your songs-in-progress, are on that very same journey.

The record business encourages us to think of music making as a start-and-stop process: each new record, released at intervals of a year or two, is a leap forward, with a batch of new ideas ready for consideration and consumption. But the reality of the musician's life is that it is one step after the other, missteps and detours and backtracks as well as forward motion. The most important thing is to keep going and to keep looking ahead rather than get discouraged by the fact that you have not yet arrived at the place where you want to be. The greatest songwriters are actually the ones who *never* arrive at that mythical place of artistic satisfaction. No matter where they are or what they achieve, they always have their eyes on the horizon.

So think of yourself as engaged in a process rather than in creating a series of final products. Consider the example of Patrick Brayer, an underground singer-songwriter who for years has been putting out self-recorded, self-released CDs called *The Secret Hits of Patrick Brayer*—at this writing, a staggering 42 volumes. He gets lost in the flow of new song ideas, and he sits down every day to document them. Once a new volume is finished, he moves on and rarely looks back.

> I get the bliss from the writing itself. Whether it's playing the guitar or writing a song lyric, it's the same spiritual experience for me, and it is the process that gets you there. It can't be taught and it can't be learned, and every successful individual has had to find his or her own way there. That's what you're thanking the artist for when you attend the concert or actually shell out for the CD.
>
> —Patrick Brayer

FACT AND FICTION

When you do music, if you're doing it right, you're constantly telling the truth or a portion of the truth. Part of a larger truth. Even when I'm telling a story in the first person that never happened to me, some part of it is the truth or I wouldn't be able to do it.

—David Bromberg

I confess, I still haven't forgiven or forgotten her. No, not a first love who left me in the lurch, but the librarian at my elementary school. I was in first grade and thoroughly jazzed about reading. At library time, I would browse the shelves and pick out some books, then bring them to the checkout desk with some trepidation, because I knew I had to pass the test: The librarian would open my selections at random, choose a couple of big words off the page, and ask me what these words meant. And if I didn't know, she wouldn't let me bring the books home. She'd send me off to find alternatives that were safely within my realm of knowledge.

I often think of this woman, and her dubious philosophy of learning, when I encounter the standard advice given to generations of writers: Write what you know. That librarian's motto was essentially the same: Read what you know. In reading, don't confuse yourself with words (or, by extension, ideas) that you don't understand; in writing, stay within your own experience. A little ambiguity or a stretch of the imagination, in other words, can be a dangerous or at least disorienting thing.

I'm thankful that my parents didn't apply the same filter to the books that we had at home or that I borrowed from the public library, so my mind was free to ponder the mysteries of words of all sizes. Even if I didn't go to the dictionary to look up the definition of a word I didn't know, I was still on some level glimpsing its meaning from the context of the story. My sense of the possibilities of language was expanding.

Similarly, I'm glad that when I sat down to write my first song, I didn't stop myself from writing the words that came out. Seen in the light of "write what you know," my lyrics were pretty absurd: I was barely a teenager, and I was writing in the first-person voice of a middle-aged father looking regretfully and melodramatically back at divorce.

I certainly wouldn't present my Opus No. 1 as being a great song. And I couldn't even tell you exactly why I was writing that particular story—my parents' marriage was intact, and I don't recall ruminating heavily on divorce and fatherhood. Most likely I was just responding to the grown-up confessional bent of the

Joni Mitchell

singer-songwriters of that era—the late '70s. For whatever reason, that sad little breakup song was what I wanted to write, instead of something about what it was like to be in seventh grade. And when I was done, I could say with plenty of satisfaction that I had written a song. I was a songwriter, and primed for Opus No. 2.

It is surely the case that someone who *had* experienced divorce directly could write a more convincing song about it than I did. This is why we get the advice to write what we know. There's an undeniable power to writing about things that we've felt or seen or smelled or touched. The details have a certain glow of authenticity, as one of the masters of turning personal experience into song once explained to me (via, naturally, a personal anecdote).

I didn't really begin to write songs until I crossed the border into the States in 1965. I had always written poetry, mostly because I had to on assignment. But I hated poetry in school; it always seemed shallow and contrived and insincere to me. All of the great poets seemed to be playing around with sonics and linguistics, but they were so afraid to express themselves without surrounding it in poetic legalese. Whenever they got sensitive, I don't know, I just didn't buy it.

When I read the philosopher Nietzsche in the '70s, I was delighted to hear what he wrote about poetry. He basically called it a lot of phony baloney through the philosopher figure Zarathustra, who was also a poet. After he has slandered the poets to the max, this disciple says, "But Zarathustra, how can you say this of the poets? Are you not also a poet?" "Of course," he says. "How else would I know?" And then he says, "But I see a new breed of poet, a penitent of spirit; they write in their own blood."

I believe to this day that if you are writing that which you know firsthand, it'll have greater vitality than if you're writing from other people's writings or secondhand information.

—Joni Mitchell

Ultimately, the problem with the advice "write what you know" is that it's often interpreted too narrowly, especially by beginning writers. There is so much that we "know" and even "know first-hand": not just the particulars of our own lives, but what we have seen others go through, what we've empathized with, what we've talked about, and what we've contemplated in our dreams. And there are no clean lines between these levels of knowledge—we are constantly relating what is inside our own experience to what is outside. The imagination loves to mix and match and play all around the blurry lines that separate fact and fiction, and the best art comes when we let it go free.

As listeners, we can't resist wondering whether stories told by our favorite artists in song are true or not. But as countless song-writers have told me over the years, the answer is typically not so clear-cut. Good songs are both personal and universal, whether you are writing in character or directly from your own life.

> *If you're writing a character that you don't understand, then you shouldn't be writing that character. You're going to be identifying with a character, and you're going to be identifying with something in you. So you're trying to find a voice that's not exactly your voice, but you're writing about feelings or emotions that you think you have an insight into.*
>
> —Paul Simon

In writing songs, when you don't hold yourself up to some pseudo-journalistic standard of what is "true," all kinds of possibilities open up. Recently I wrote a song that was sparked by a rhythm beaten out on a table and the view of a big, beautiful sycamore tree outside the window. *Sycamore* has a great rhythm and became the basis of a chorus. I started imagining someone growing up in a house next to a sycamore tree and relating stages of childhood back to that tree. The boy in my story remains for-ever attached to the sycamore tree, even after he's grown up and moved away and his parents have sold the house. At the end, the song shifts from third person to first person—as *I* drive back to that house, with a family of my own in the car, to see the sycamore tree once more.

So, is this a true story? This sycamore tree is outside my house right now, but I have only lived here a couple of years. This city is full of people who have stayed very close to where they grew up, who are surrounded by extended family and lifelong friends. I envy their rootedness and feel like a carpetbagger by comparison, even as I've enjoyed exploring different parts of the country. But my parents still live in my childhood home, so I have a taste of what it's like to relate to a particular place throughout life, and I want my children to know what that's like too. All these feelings were somehow transferred onto the image of the sycamore tree, and they fed into a story that is not "true"—it didn't happen to me—but is nonetheless true, on a deeper level, to what I feel and think about.

I didn't set out to write a song about what it means to have roots and to leave them behind. I just followed where the story and the music were leading me. By starting in third person and leaving behind the chronology and particulars of my life, I wound up writing something that revealed much more about my emotions and longings than I ever intended.

A lot of times when you're writing in first person or what you think is first person— a sort of autobiographical song—when the song is done it is pretty much fiction. And some of the songs in the voice of a character, where I thought I was telling someone else's story, actually turn out to have a lot more autobiography in them.... When you're writing songs that are autobiographical, you're always writing about what you know about yourself, just like if you write about a character, you're writing about what you know about that character. It's kind of a tip-of-the-iceberg deal: a lot of stuff that you don't know you're putting into songs actually gets in there.

I like what Tom Waits says about songwriting: Just because something is true doesn't mean that it's interesting. I think that's a real good thing to keep in mind. It doesn't really matter whether the story is mine or somebody I know or something I imagined. If you write a song that's autobiographical in a closed-off way, in a diary sort of way, where it's too personal, too self-involved—that song is not going to communicate to anybody. If you write a song about something that you're dealing with that lots of other people are dealing with, too, then it can jump that gap and communicate. The only thing I think really matters in a song is, does it communicate? Is there room for other people to bring their hearts to it? Is there room for you to come in and kick off your shoes? If there is, then it's a good song.

—Greg Brown

IN SEARCH OF STYLE

A distinctive style is a musician's most prized possession. It's what allows listeners to recognize an artist within just a few notes of a song that they have never heard before. Style isn't so much *what* is being expressed in a song as *how* it is being expressed: a special quality of tone, phrasing, image, melody, or groove—or a combination of elements—that distinguishes one artist from all the others who are working with the same source material. For a singer-songwriter, a style of your own has a tremendous long-term value; it helps people to know and remember you beyond whatever particular song might have first caught their attention, and it provides a natural starting point for your songwriting now and down the road.

Sounds great, but how do you find this elusive thing called style? Are you just born with it, or do you discover it through sweat and determination and luck, like some sort of buried treasure?

Greg Brown

Certainly one aspect of developing your own style is looking outside of yourself—pushing yourself into new territory and learning new chops. But as Suzanne Vega once memorably explained, there's another way to look at style: not as what you do in your music, but as what you *don't* do.

I prefer short words to long ones, because I find that's the quickest way to get someone's attention. If you say, "My name is Luka / I live on the second floor," you're drawn into this picture because it's such specific, concrete information and the language is so simple. But the funny thing was that two years ago I found out that I was an asthmatic—I had never been diagnosed as having asthma. When I mentioned this to my drummer, he laughed and said he figured there was a reason why I had such short phrases. I have short words, short phrases; I don't stand around holding the note

out or using any vibrato because I can't—I have no breath! So I
guess it's all developed in a way that suits my style. I mean it
sounds kind of pathetic, but it isn't, really: Developing a style
means finding out where your limits are and making the best of
them.

—Suzanne Vega

So instead of imagining a treasure hunt, think of finding your own style as chipping away at a block of stone until you sculpt a face out of it. The raw material is all there in front of you; it just needs to be given shape and personality, rendered by an artistic hand. The individual style comes in your choices of what to leave out and what to emphasize, song by song by song.

I'm often impressed by singers who seem to be able to inhabit any song from any genre; they could sing the ingredients on a shampoo bottle and make them sound stirring and lyrical. I envy that versatility, especially when I'm trying to work up a cover of a favorite song that sounds hopelessly lame coming out of my mouth. But I also know that as a songwriter I have a different kind of asset: a body of music that is tailor-made for my voice. I slip so comfortably into my own songs precisely because in the writing process I have made an end run around my limitations— I've mined my own style. In terms of technique, that brilliant vocalist could sing circles around me even in my own tune. But the fact is that my song and I have a special bond that nobody else can have. That relationship is one of the prime attractions of being a singer-songwriter.

Even so, in writing songs, it's not always a good thing to stay comfortably within your limitations. When you are writing an original work, you are by definition stretching beyond what you or others have done before. You don't want to rehash or be entirely predictable. In short, you want to learn something when you write.

So how do you make the most of your limitations without being confined by your limitations? By constantly pushing against them, as Jerry Garcia described in a conversation just a few years before his death. The topic was actually improvising, but the same dynamic applies to writing songs; improvisation, he pointed out, is really just "fast composition."

> *If you've got a recognizable style, that's really your limitations, you know what I mean? Basically, you play what you know how to play. And then within that, sometimes in moments of great clarity, you are able to see stuff that you don't know how to play, but it's close enough to what you do know how to play that you might try for it, and sometimes you might hit it. I tend to do that more often than is probably safe, because I frequently fuck up. Sometimes it works, and if you keep on trying at it, eventually your percentages do improve; but then it just becomes new stuff that you do know how to play.*
>
> —Jerry Garcia

In songwriting terms, that "new stuff that you do know how to play" is your new work. Each song builds on what came before but adds a few phrases and moves to the vocabulary of your style. And what Garcia said of the hits/misses percentages holds true for songwriting as well. You have to allow yourself to fail, and the more you try, the more success you will find.

COMMERCIAL CONSIDERATIONS

All this talk about songwriting process and originality and style is fine, but what about the bottom line: Will it sell?

If only there were a simple and reliable answer to that question— the jobs of record executives, managers, publishers, artists, and everyone else in the music business would be so much more straightforward. People could choose a comfortable spot along the spectrum from commercial music on one end to "heart music" on the other, and then reap predictable rewards for the bank account and the soul.

The problem is, the marketplace is always changing, and nobody knows exactly how or why. Music-business people hate to admit this, but commercially driven decisions about the content of music mostly come down to doggedly following last week's trends, which could just as easily turn out to be the end of something as the beginning of something. The second application of a so-called proven formula looks like, well, a formula, and so loses all its power. Music is not chemistry, and the music business is not a controlled laboratory.

That means that an idea of what sells is a very rickety foundation on which to base your music. Maybe you're right about what will sell, but if you're wrong, what are you left with? As a developing singer-songwriter, what you need more than anything is to find your

James Taylor

own groove, to gain a confident sense of who you are musically and what you have to say. Trying to second-guess the marketplace will inevitably confuse and distract you from that process, as a legendary singer-songwriter with a rocky youth once pointed out to me.

My musical style developed really in a vacuum. It developed in North Carolina with a lot of time on my hands—empty, open time—and I think that's true of a lot of musicians who develop their own thing. It takes a lot of time to practice, and it takes a certain amount of alienation to want to do that instead of wanting to do social things. It means that you in some way are cut off. It's always a funny and, I think, jarring thing when you bring these things to market, when it starts to be something that happens in a public context. It's a very iffy transition for a lot of players.... The marketing side is taken very seriously and gets a lot of attention and a lot of interest. It's validated, and it eats your music—it eats it up.

—James Taylor

Even experienced musicians who manage a reasonable transition from private to public spheres, from personal expression to commercial product, struggle to maintain their musical sense of self as they deal with the vagaries of the marketplace. It's depressingly common for artists who have found commercial success to flounder creatively when they fall out of favor in the music business, as just about everyone does sooner or later. Their music has been devalued in the marketplace, and they have lost sight of its value outside of what can be expressed in unit sales and dollars.

No one should go into music as a career with the starry-eyed notion that all that matters is the art, that the business side will just take care of itself. Of course the business matters, and bad business decisions can straitjacket your creativity just as good business decisions can set your creativity free. Once you turn your music into your profession, art and business can never be completely separated.

So how is a musician supposed to operate in the marketplace without being devoured and discarded by it? Steve Seskin, who's found a lot of commercial success as a Nashville songwriter in addition to performing his own music, said the key is to build a protective wall around the creative process.

> I have this notion that you can mix art and commerce quite well, but that you shouldn't let the commerce poison the art. I just believe that you should create whatever you create, and then figure out how to sell it after it's done. What's wrong with that? We don't have to play starving musician our whole lives.
>
> In Nashville, there are a lot of writers who will sit down, and on the blackboard behind them is the cut chart of who is cutting next month and what kind of songs they are looking for. I'd rather sit down and write a song with somebody that's what we feel like doing that day, and write the best song we can write, and then try to figure out who's looking and who we can pitch it to.
>
> —Steve Seskin

Darrell Scott, another successful Nashville songsmith with a long-running solo career, sounded a similar note when I asked if he has any idea during the writing process whether a song might be pitchable to another artist.

> If I'm thinking of that while I am writing a song, the song is probably sucking, because the best songs are about being true to what the song wants to be. I have no agenda whatsoever that I'm going to steer it country or I'm going to steer it poppy. I've played in country music all my life, but if I have a song that wants to be really bluegrass or really mountain, I just simply go where the song wants to go. And the odd thing to me is the songs I've had the biggest cuts on are the ones that I was totally writing for myself. I'm still amazed that major country acts have wanted to do those, and I just think the bottom line is they wanted to say what I said on my own and for myself.
>
> —Darrell Scott

When you try to write songs according to a commercial formula or targeting a particular market/star, you overlook your greatest strengths: your own identity and point of view. And you risk losing touch with what James Taylor called "the source"—the reason you got into this business in the first place.

> *Just play your music, and do it for the people who love it for music. In other words, play it in public, play it in private for people who love it, go on the road with it, play it for other musicians, and try to minimize the extent to which you are playing it for someone's marketing scheme, to accommodate somebody's idea of how to sell it and how to move it as a product. That's confusing, and that's not the point. It exists for an emotional reason and not for a commercial one, primarily.*
>
> —James Taylor

ON THE DRAWING BOARD

It's such a subconscious thing. It's like this little song part of you fills up over time. It's like a well, and then you just put your dipper in and dip it out. When you're a songwriter, at least a songwriter like me, you have to work hard on your craft—if you hear something, you want to be able to figure out how to do it. But the songs themselves, I don't know where they come from or where they're going or why they picked me. They really are presents, and your job is to receive them and pass them on.

—Greg Brown

Ask songwriters where their ideas come from, and they grope for the right words or image to explain the essentially inexplicable: Songs just appear out of the blue, like lightning on a sunny day. They are forever floating past us, available to anyone who's listening. They spring from interesting mistakes and lucky accidents, and, of course, from private pain and emotional turmoil. They are like fish down in the dark waters, sometimes taking your bait and sometimes not. Inspiration is a mysterious thing, and oftentimes songwriters don't even want to penetrate that mystery—they fear that if they understand what is going on, they won't be able to tap into it anymore.

Inspiration may be impossible to define or control or predict, but that doesn't mean that we have to just sit around idly waiting for it. As we will explore in this chapter, there are many ways in which we can make ourselves more receptive to inspiration and quicker to recognize it when it comes. We can tune our ears and continually open them to new sounds. We can raise the odds that the right kinds of accidents will occur. And, as Greg Brown suggested, we can hone our craft, so that we have the necessary skills to translate what we hear and bring it to life with our own vocal cords and instruments.

What we call the songwriting process isn't really one process; it's an aggregation of processes. Songs begin life in endlessly varied ways and usually go through multiple stages—some completely unconscious, some very much driven by conscious intent—on their way to completion. The process that works for one song won't necessarily apply to the next one. The best thing we can do is be open and ready for all possibilities.

There are three different musical worlds that go on in my life at once. There's the dimension of songwriting that is crafting the melodies and lyrics at all times. I've got a hundred pieces of paper, scraps, hotel stationery, and then a constant work-in-progress Walkman tape. Then there's the other side of me that just writes songs in one sitting at one time—it's the straight, lightning-bolt channel. And then right in the center there's the stream of consciousness, and I'll just sit down and ramble and write five pages of garbage. For my songwriting, that's the trinity.

—Ben Harper

When asked about songwriting, Pete Seeger likes to quote Thomas Edison's dictum that genius is 1 percent inspiration and 99 percent perspiration. It is surely true that a flash of inspiration makes all the sweat worthwhile; it's also true that all the sweat makes it possible to receive the inspiration in the first place. Let's look at both sides of this remarkable and complex process, from idea to finished song.

Fishing for Ideas

Over the years, scores of singer-songwriters have shared with me the approaches and tricks that help them find new songs and break through those dreaded periods of writer's block. Here's a compendium of ideas from those conversations. Not every one will make sense to you, but you might be surprised by how well your muse responds to the right kind of coaxing.

❖ ***Babble.*** If you ever write music before words, chances are you sing nonsense phrases or just raw sounds that happen to fit the melody and rhythm. Usually you need to get rid of this stuff and write "real" words (we're all glad that Paul McCartney came up with "yesterday" to replace his original words, "scrambled eggs"), but pay attention to what is burbling up from your subconscious. Sometimes it'll point you in an interesting direction, and besides, these words or sounds are beautifully matched with the music—that's why you sang them in the first place. Try babbling into a recorder or onto paper, just letting it flow without editing or filtering. You can look back later for usable ideas or just toss out the whole thing.

> The process for me is usually sitting down, hitting the chord, starting to throw my voice into the chord, keeping a tape recorder going the whole time because I get into a sort of trance where I am stumbling around in melody land. I don't know what I'm doing. I just start singing nonsense syllables, and a word will form. Later on when I finish the song, I can go back to that work tape, and nine times out of ten the vowel sounds have already started to become

what ends up being the line a month later or two months later. I
really believe that there's this subconscious soup that everything is
formed in, where there's a greater wisdom than my pea brain can
offer me.

—Beth Nielsen Chapman

This kind of writing is fun to do in tandem, too. Try a space jam with another instrumentalist, just exploring sounds without any notion of what key you're in or what you're going to play, and record the results. Or sit with a friend in a noisy, crowded room (like a bar—anyplace where it's hard to concentrate) and write spontaneous verse back and forth, a few lines at a time. No pausing allowed. By shutting down your thought process, you might come up with some strange, funny, and compelling ideas.

I often feel most fulfilled by my own things when I don't know
what I'm writing about at first. I just get something that I believe in
enough to sing to and mumble into a Walkman, and listen back to
what I'm trying to get at without deliberating words. And then you
start getting an idea. It comes around to making beautiful stuff
out of junk, out of nothing, something Zen-ish.

—Chris Whitley

❖ *Make mistakes.* Many guitar-playing songwriters have gotten hooked on using alternate tunings because a new tuning undercuts what they know how to play and creates an environment for weird and interesting accidents. That's just one example of how mistakes can generate great ideas and why they are worth cultivating.

If you're only working off what you know, then you can't grow. It's
only through error that discovery is made, and in order to discover
you have to set up some sort of situation with a random element,
a strange attractor, using contemporary physics terms. The more I

can surprise myself, the more I'll stay in this business, and the twid-
dling of the notes is one way to keep the pilgrimage going. You're
constantly pulling the rug out from under yourself, so you don't get
a chance to settle into any kind of formula.

—Joni Mitchell

Chris Whitley

❖ *Eavesdrop and observe.* If you are paying attention, everywhere you go you'll find intriguing details that can be the starting points for constructing whole stories and characters. Who would put a bumper sticker that says "Worms Eat My Garbage" on their car? What was that woman at the café saying about door-to-door plastic surgery in L.A.? What's the story with that sad-looking man who trims his lawn with a pair of scissors? Try writing a song from the point of view of someone you saw at the laundromat or overheard trying to impress a dinner date. Be a detective, and take good notes: specific words and precise images.

❖ *Give yourself an assignment.* Even if you never liked doing homework in school, you might get a lot of productivity and pleasure from giving yourself songwriting assignments. Look at your repertoire and try to write something a little different: a song with a particular rhyme scheme, a sweet and slow one to balance all your hard-charging songs, an epic ballad based on a newspaper story, a song with an unreliable narrator, a song with only two chords, a song with no chorus . . . Sometimes it's even better to get an assignment from someone else—the kind of thing you never would have come up with. New York's Fast Folk collective has been doing this effectively for years (sample assignment: write a love song with the word *elevator* in it). Challenging yourself like this gets a different part of your brain involved in the process— the part that likes doing puzzles or figuring out Web-page code— and can be very energizing.

❖ *Get away from your instrument.* No matter what instrument you play, your songwriting is dependent on your instrumental ability. One sure-fire way to get past your technical limitations is to not play at all. Sing while you're walking or driving; motion and changing scenery always seem to be good for sparking the imagination. Improvise over a rhythm beaten out on your chest or on the dashboard, or over a drum loop. There are two big advantages to doing this: if you just sing, the odds are high that you will come up with the elusive thing called a singable melody, which sounds great just by itself; and chances are, you will write something much simpler (melodically and lyrically) than you would otherwise allow yourself to write—sitting there with your instrument, that tune would probably seem too obvious to pursue. And when you do add some kind of accompaniment, you can do so with an ear to what the melody really needs, rather than be locked into a chord progression you came up with first.

A lot of times I don't even need the guitar to write. In fact, sometimes the guitar can get in the way, because it'll stop the flow of where the song is going in my head.

—Tish Hinojosa

❖ *Expand your instrumental technique.* New capabilities on your instrument will surely lead you to new songs. So you might explore a new style or repertoire, take some lessons or a workshop, pick up an instruction book or songbook or video. If you are a guitar player and strum with a pick, consider learning some fingerstyle techniques, or experiment with alternate tunings. Study jazz standards or fiddle tunes. You don't have to become a hotshot shredder—the aim is just to open up new possibilities for your writing. Strong instrumental chops are not only good for songwriting but are a major (and often undervalued) asset for performing. If you play by yourself, your accompaniment is half of your sound.

❖ *Try a different instrument.* If you can really learn your way around a second instrument, more power to you. On record and onstage, playing even one or two songs on a different instrument livens up your sound considerably. But it can be fun and fruitful to try writing even on an instrument that you don't know how to play or barely know how to play. You have an enviable kind of freedom when you have no idea what you're doing, and you can use that freedom to generate ideas. Within the stringed-instrument family alone, there are many options, from bouzoukis to mandolins to ukuleles, so go explore. Lately I've been writing a bit on a Strumstick, an odd little three-stringed instrument that's made a few cameos in pop music (Jennifer Kimball, Tracy Chapman). I've come up with some distinctive and cool-sounding parts, but the funny thing is, when I've translated them over to the guitar (my main instrument) they sound really ordinary. In other words, the Strumstick is leading me to songs I would have passed by otherwise.

Jill Sobule described how switch-hitting on drums once helped her break a case of writer's block.

When I would start playing my guitar, I got really bored with it. I would start going to the same chords, the same rhythms, and I think I had to put my guitar away and find a new instrument. Once I did that I came back to my guitar and it become fresh again, and I tried to work on things like new tunings, learning more—more tools to write.

—Jill Sobule

❖ *Switch media.* All the art forms arise from the same basic impulses, and you can take songwriting inspiration from any medium—poetry, novels, painting, sculpture, professional wrestling . . . Since you are working with words, books are a natural place to look for ideas on how to use language and imagery and develop memorable characters.

My own life is rich enough with disaster and metaphor to write from that, but when I am reading a book, a phrase or a line or a word just sets me off and makes my mind reel. I'll write it down and think about it, and I'll go write something on my own and come back and read. I'm constantly getting sent off in different directions by somebody's writing.

—Jennifer Kimball

Several singer-songwriters have also described to me how working in another medium, like the visual arts, refreshes and improves their songwriting.

I really like writing and drawing, and I get bored doing one thing too long. It's sort of like if you are a farmer and you plant the same crop every year, it depletes the soil, but if you rotate crops it puts nutrients back in the soil, so when you go back to the same crop, it makes it stronger. For me, writing is like that. If I switch from songwriting to poetry, my songwriting gets better in my absence. Whereas if I do it all the time, it just burns me out. I don't get any new information that makes my songwriting better. Sometimes just doing visual art, concentrating on pure shapes for the sake of shapes, makes my melody writing better. It makes my phrasing stronger.

—Jewel

❖ **Learn other people's songs.** Many of us learn to play by looping our favorite songs over and over, instrument in hand, and that's a great way to inspire yourself at any stage. Getting inside somebody else's song craft expands your songwriting vocabulary and your sense of possibilities. If you want to learn someone's track note for note, go for it; but I think it can be even more illuminating to rely on your ears and your hands and come up with your own rendition or to adapt a part from a different instrument so you *can't* reproduce it exactly. It's amazing how often artists write great songs by failing to play someone else's song accurately.

❖ **Listen to new music.** This seems obvious, but check out artists or genres you don't know very well, that are far from your musical home base. It's almost better if you have no chance of ever sounding like whatever you're hearing; that way, you can freely steal ideas without worrying about plagiarism. These days, it's easy to sample new music in record stores before dropping a lot of money for the disc, and of course the Web is a global bazaar of music for free and for sale. Experiencing a new artist in person, rather than just on record, can give you an even clearer sense of what makes the music tick. Festivals with eclectic lineups are a perfect place to check out a wide variety of live music without committing yourself to a full performance by an act you may or may not like.

❖ *Imagine an audience.* I picked up this intriguing idea from pop/folk singer-songwriter Catie Curtis.

> *I don't do well trying to write in the voice of another artist. I get bummed out. It works better for me to try to imagine playing for one of my favorite artists' audiences. I guess it's similar, but it allows me to do it my way. If the audience loves cool guitar riffs and dark humor (à la Richard Thompson), I picture them as I try to write something. Dar Williams has such a smart, attentive, progressive audience. Several times I've written songs motivated by knowing I'd be playing gigs with her. If I wrote imagining Joan Armatrading's audience, I'd feel safe writing a heart-wrenching love ballad. So I get inspired by the aesthetic of the artist, but I try to stay in my own voice.*
>
> —Catie Curtis

❖ *Arrange and rearrange.* If the silence is deafening and you're tired of staring at a blank page, try working with existing material. Write lyrics to a favorite melody, or set some favorite lyrics or poetry to a new melody. If you hope to use the results professionally without jumping through a lot of hoops, stick to public domain sources (e.g., a traditional folk song, an old classical melody or poem), but it can still be a great exercise to rewrite a pop hit or otherwise mess around with copyrighted material for your own edification and amusement. The process of adapting forces you to stretch outside yourself and solve problems creatively. Here's how Duncan Sheik described the process of setting Stephen Sater's poetry to music for the album *Phantom Moon*.

> Usually I write music first and then words later, whenever they come to me. So it was a little bit of an adjustment, but once I got into the process it became very natural. In fact I really enjoyed it, because it becomes this kind of fascinating puzzle, how you can make a line of text work as a musical phrase, and how you can take the structure of the given text and make that work as a musical structure in terms of the whole song. It became its own little adventure each time.
>
> —Duncan Sheik

If you have trouble breaking free from one particular version of your source material (say, you're trying to write new words to "Over the Rainbow" but can't get Judy Garland's image out of your head), try speeding it way up or slowing it way down, transposing it to a different key or to a different instrument—anything to make the familiar seem strange and new.

❖ *Use a "ghost writer."* You may not be able to call up your favorite artists and invite them to collaborate, but that shouldn't stop you from setting up a virtual songwriting partnership in your head. A few months back I was playing around with a guitar groove and melody that reminded me of Steve Earle's gritty ballads, so I imagined him (black T-shirt, skull tattoo, and all) singing my fledgling tune and tried to hear what he was singing about. On other occasions I've done the same thing with Tom Waits, and he's led me down a back alley I wouldn't have found otherwise.

Spooky? Sure, but effective—especially because I'm constitution-
ally incapable of sounding like these guys. In addition to imagining what a particular artist would do with your song-in-progress,
you might conjure a collaboration between two artists who never
could or would be in the same room together.

❖ *Collaborate (for real).* Of course, there are advantages to having a flesh-and-blood collaborator, whether a full-fledged co-
writer or just someone you can bounce ideas off (more on these
topics later in this chapter). I have broken quite a few logjams in
my own songwriting by soliciting an off-the-cuff reaction to what
I was working on from someone nearby—and he or she does not
have to be a musician. Sing your embryonic melody and ask,
"What does it sound like this song should be about?" Or read your
verses and ask, "What should happen next in this story?"

❖ *Join a songwriting group.* Songwriting organizations are
ubiquitous these days, and they can be well worth joining. They
provide a place to get informed feedback, moral support, and performing experience, and an upcoming meeting or open-mic showcase adds a healthy bit of deadline pressure to finish that song
you're working on. As mentioned above, the group might even
prod your creativity with songwriting assignments. Don't be
intimidated by the prospect of being judged by your peers; in my
experience, songwriting groups foster cooperation rather than
competition. Connecting with your local music community is
beneficial in so many ways, whether you are looking for a co-
writer, a bass player to play on a demo, or someone to share the
bill at a coffeehouse.

❖ *Just do it.* In Nashville, there are staff writers who literally go
to the office and write songs nine to five, 40 hours a week, 48
weeks a year. Even if you can't imagine creating according to that

kind of corporate time clock, you might benefit from developing some sort of songwriting routine: sitting down for a defined period of time and just doing it, as a writer sits down at the keyboard or a painter sits at the easel. If you passively wait for the muse to strike, said Ed Robertson of Barenaked Ladies, there are "movies to see and food to eat and places to go." A songwriting regimen removes some of the pressure that can build up during a dry spell; instead of fretting about the weather, you're honing your craft and preparing yourself for the moment when the sky finally opens.

> I think that writers should write at times other than when they feel like it. You can inject discipline into it, but the key is not to have expectations of how much you are going to produce during that time, because songwriting is just not like hanging Sheetrock, where your boss expects you to have hung a certain amount of Sheetrock in the eight hours that you worked. Songwriting can't be judged that way. Allan Shamblin and I wrote "Don't Laugh at Me" in about four hours. Well, we got really lucky that day. We have another story song called "Cactus in a Coffee Can" that took probably 100 hours over a six-month period to write, because it just wasn't right. So if we get together for six hours and we come up with one line that we love, that's still a good day.
>
> —Steve Seskin

THE SONGWRITER'S TOOL KIT

You don't *need* anything to write a song, but there are tools (aside from your instrument and its accessories) that can come in very handy. Let's take a look at what you might want to have in your tool kit.

❖ *Idea book.* As the old adage goes, a writer is one on whom nothing is lost. Consider yourself a reporter and a scavenger, collecting every notable idea that pops up and filing away all the intriguing details observed and overheard in your daily travels. An English teacher of mine suggested visualizing a lazy Susan (one of those kitchen-table trays that spins around to pass the salt and pepper) on which you place interesting notions that you don't quite know what to do with yet, so they are stowed away yet remain within easy reach. As a writer, you should have a mental storage system such as this, and use hard copy to back it up.

Many writers wind up scribbling notes on scraps and napkins that eventually disappear in the cracks of the car seat or laundry machine or who knows where. A small notebook with a pen attached, or perhaps index cards and a system for storing them, can help preserve these ideas in their pure and original form, rather than as how you kinda sorta remember them. (Be sure to write your name and phone number on your notebook, too, so it might find its way back to you if you leave it on a café table!)

A notebook is of obvious use for lyric ideas (phrases, images, couplets), but it's even handier if you can train yourself to jot down a snippet of melody. Pete Seeger told me he has retained many middle-of-the-night inspirations this way.

❖ *Recorder.* Every songwriter should have a recorder of some sort—quick to access, simple to use, and easy to take with you wherever you go. Your recorder is the audio equivalent of the idea book; use it to capture cool bits and pieces of music you happen upon and might use someday. And when you are farther along in writing a song, record yourself and listen back to gain some perspective and figure out where you still have work to do.

The portable cassette recorder has been a ubiquitous musician's tool for many years, but there are good reasons to consider going digital. The sound quality on a portable digital recorder such as the minidisc can be remarkably good even with a cheap lapel mic, and it's very handy to be able to edit out stuff you don't need and to have instant access to things you do need. I have boxes full of old work tapes that I never listen to simply because it's too tedious to make my way through a 90-minute cassette for the three minutes I actually want to hear.

There are many excellent and inexpensive digital multitrack machines available, and for some types of songs it's very useful to hear a drum loop or a bass line under your accompaniment part. But don't sacrifice portability and simplicity for whiz-bang technology. And don't let the recording process divert you from the more important business of writing the best song you possibly can, as the producer and engineer Malcolm Burn (Bob Dylan, Emmylou Harris, Chris Whitley) once noted.

> *I think there's something to be said for really focusing on your songwriting and not being distracted by making elaborate demos. The more time you've been doing that, the less time you spend figuring out what it is you are trying to say. Diddling around with a snare sound or something like that is not songwriting.*
>
> —Malcolm Burn

❖ **Beatbox.** Drum machines and drum-loop generators, both stand-alone boxes and software, are being used by more and more songwriters these days. Starting with a rhythm and then adding chords and melody is a very different process from working the other way around in the traditional fashion, and obviously it lends itself very well to beat-oriented pop-music styles (that is, just about all styles of pop music). It's a common weakness in songs for the melody to be too closely tied to the chord progression, and improvising a melody over a drum pattern can be an effective way to achieve stronger, more independent melodies. Likewise, chord progressions that are composed first are often busier than they need to be; starting with a drum part can lead to leaner and better accompaniment.

Similar caveats apply to working with a drum machine as to using a multitrack recorder. Don't get so consumed by the technology and the recorded sound that you shortchange your song craft and wind up with what Ed Robertson called "no song hidden behind fantastic production." And treat a drum loop as you would any other instrument part—as something to refine and revise and perhaps leave behind. No matter what tools you use, *you*—not your tools—have to guide the songwriting process.

❖ *Books.* Songwriters are wordsmiths, and your bookshelf should contain some of the same reference books that prose and poetry writers use: a dictionary, of course, plus a thesaurus for finding alternatives to overly familiar or already used words, and a rhyming dictionary for breaking free of "blues/lose/shoes" rhymes. These reference works are available in electronic form as well, if that better suits your working style. There's also a huge selection of advice-oriented books for writers that is worth checking out. See Resources for a few of my personal faves.

❖ *Computer.* Wired singer-songwriters will find many resources available on their own PCs and over the Web. There is specialized software for songwriters, both for keeping track of lyrics and chords and for organizing your business dealings. (For listings of software and Web sites, see Resources.) Here are a few examples of what you can find on the Internet: songwriting and performance-rights organizations, announcements of contests and events, copyright information and forms, lyrics and chords (though not always accurate) for just about any song you can think of, vast and fully searchable song databases (wondering if that great title has been used before?), guitar and keyboard lessons, chord-generating software, chat rooms and message boards and tips sheets . . . As with all things on the Web, the offerings are overwhelming, and you have to dig through a lot of dirt to locate each gem of a resource.

Just make sure you spend enough time off-line that you actually write and perform some songs!

Understanding Theory and Form

"Uh-oh," you're thinking as you look for the nearest exit, "the *th* word!"

Musicians outside the jazz and classical realms have sharply divided opinions on the value of understanding the theory and mechanics of music. Some react to the whole subject with a mixture of dread and guilt, as if they have just been caught snoozing in the back row of a deadly boring class. For others, theoretical knowledge is simply irrelevant to the way they look at music.

> It took me a long time to learn. I found it not by theory but just by my heart, by sounds, and I had to make all these decisions about how to play the guitar just based on what I heard. Sometimes it was to soothe me, so it would be this kind of a monotonous journey; I would play the same chords over and over and over. I wanted to know emotionally everything about the chord that I was playing.
>
> I remember wrapping myself down around the guitar and putting my ear on top of the body and playing the notes. I think probably I was intoxicated by the harmonics but didn't know that that's what it was. I really didn't know if what I was playing was a chord; I would just decide if what I was playing matched. And I would decide it by my ear and my feelings. Of course I see now that there would have been a much easier way to do it.
>
> Looking back on it now—I wouldn't have had the words for it then—I was deeply trying to understand why anybody would go from a D major to an E minor. And emotionally the distance between those two chords is all the reason why you'd then write a song. So anytime I'd learn a new chord I would write a song. It's as if I was a bag of candy, and when I got a new chord the bag would

just get smashed open; and then I would write a series of songs
using this chord in a particular way following a particular emotion
that had occurred from learning it.

—Ferron

Songwriting should come from the ear and the heart, one line of
argument goes, and learning too much about how music is con-
ventionally put together dooms you to write songs that are, well,
conventional. Dave Matthews's songs are so distinctive, his duo
partner Tim Reynolds said, because he hasn't had "chord progres-

Paul Simon

sions shoved down [his] throat." Patty Larkin and others have described how they had to almost unlearn jazz theory in order to write more rootsy songs.

I once posed the question to Paul Simon: Could learning music theory be a trap for a songwriter, in that if you're aware of all these possibilities, you might feel you have to use them?

> *I don't think it's a trap. Simple is always a choice. . . . How you hear music, what your instinct is, is going to be how you express music. When you want to express something that's more complex, it would be nice to have that available to you. And there are times when just the simplest of chords is going to be the most satisfying, and you want to know that that moment has arrived. I think the more technique that you have, the more options you have of expressing yourself. I mean how you express yourself is your nature, so it may be very moving, it may be artistic, and it may be banal, but it's not because you had too much knowledge.*
>
> —Paul Simon

Here's another perspective, from Chris Thile of the band Nickel Creek, who, like most bluegrass-rooted musicians, learned to play strictly by ear but later spent a few college semesters studying composition and theory.

> *I thoroughly enjoyed it and learned so much during that time, and I'm trying to keep going. It's all in the interest of being a well-rounded musician. I especially admire the composers—they have so much control over their ideas and how to reproduce them with an orchestra or string quartet or solo piano or whatever. It's a completely different thing than a jazz-style arrangement, where you direct, but the musicians you choose have a lot of control over their own parts. It's just another way to learn.*
>
> —Chris Thile

My own music education consisted of lots of hunting and pecking on the guitar, guided by songbooks and obsessive looping of my favorite records, and a little bit of formal study. I've come to the conclusion that there is no substitute for a good ear, but that music theory is a) not nearly as difficult to learn as people assume it is and b) very useful even in small doses. In Resources I've recommended a few places to look for detailed explanations of music theory and song form, but let's look at a few simple concepts of particular relevance to songwriters. I won't get into note reading or other fundamentals here, but will instead focus on chords and how they fit together.

❖ *Chords in a key.* Again and again I've heard beginning songwriters ask the question: How do you know which chords sound good together in a song? The answer starts with the *major scale:* a sequence of notes that you will recognize as *do re mi fa sol la ti do* (go rent *The Sound of Music* and sing along with "Do-Re-Mi" if you need a refresher). The first note of the scale is called the *root* (or simply the 1), and then we step up the scale by degrees until we arrive again at the root an *octave* higher (the same note at a higher frequency). Here's what the major scale looks like starting at the note *C*—otherwise known as a *C* major scale.

do	re	mi	fa	sol	la	ti	do
C	D	E	F	G	A	B	C
1	2	3	4	5	6	7	8 (or 1)

We create this *do re mi* sound by following a specific pattern of *intervals,* or distances between notes. In a major scale, we always have the following sequence of whole steps (on a guitar, the equivalent of two frets) and half steps (one fret).

do	re	mi	fa	sol	la	ti	do
C	D	E	F	G	A	B	C
1	2	3	4	5	6	7	8 (or 1)

Whole Whole Half Whole Whole Whole Half

By starting on any note and following the same pattern of whole and half steps, we can create a major scale in any key.

Scales aren't devised by music teachers (or authors) to bore you to tears. They are the building blocks of both melodies (for example, a simple song in the key of C will use mostly or entirely notes in the C major scale) and chords. We can build a chord off of each note in the scale using other notes in the scale and, presto, arrive at the basic chords in a key. Take a look at this chart of the chords in major keys. The Roman numerals in the top row indicate which degree of the scale the chord is built on, as well as the type of chord: uppercase Roman numerals are used for major chords, and lowercase for minor and diminished chords. The I is the tonic chord and also the name of the key.

Major Keys

I	ii	iii	IV	V or V7	vi	vii
C	Dm	Em	F	G or G7	Am	Bdim
D♭	E♭m	Fm	G♭	A♭ or A♭7	B♭m	Cdim
D	Em	F♯m	G	A or A7	Bm	C♯dim
E♭	Fm	Gm	A♭	B♭ or B♭7	Cm	Ddim
E	F♯m	G♯m	A	B or B7	C♯m	D♯dim
F	Gm	Am	B♭	C or C7	Dm	Edim
G♭	A♭m	B♭m	B	D♭ or D♭7	E♭m	Fdim
G	Am	Bm	C	D or D7	Em	F♯dim
A♭	B♭m	Cm	D♭	E♭ or E♭7	Fm	Gdim
A	Bm	C♯m	D	E or E7	F♯m	G♯dim
B♭	Cm	Dm	E♭	F or F7	Gm	Adim
B	C♯m	D♯m	E	F♯ or F♯7	G♯m	A♯dim

Notice that no matter what key we're in, the I, IV, and V chords are major; the ii, iii, and vi chords are minor; and the vii is a diminished chord.

If your eyes are getting bleary, block out the sharp and flat keys and also ignore the infrequently used vii diminished chords. Guitarists, focus on the friendly keys with the most open chords (which are shaded in the charts): *C, D, E, G,* and *A.* Some of these chords crop up much more often in songs than others. The I is our most important chord—it's our harmonic home base, the place where the song's journey begins and ends (unless the composer is intentionally leaving things more ambiguous). Then comes the V or V7 chord, which always wants to resolve to the I: think of the four-part "a-aa-aaa-aaah" vocal crescendo in "Twist and Shout," building a V7 chord, and how sweet it is when it resolves to the I with "Shake it up, baby." Some songs use nothing more than the I and V ("Jambalaya," "Iko Iko").

Add in the IV chord, and you've got all you need to play thousands of songs—the I, IV, and V are the bricks and mortar of blues, rock, country, and folk. The next most common chord would be the vi (just think of how many songs in the key of *C* include an *Am*). So if you are writing a song in the key of *C,* you could refer to this chart for other likely chords to use: the IV (*F*) and V (*G*) for sure, plus the vi (*Am*) and the other chords in the *C* row. Handy, eh?

We can go through the exact same process with the minor keys, starting with the *natural minor scale.* (We actually find the natural minor scale by starting on the sixth degree of a major scale and going up to the sixth an octave higher. The sixth note of a *C* major scale is *A,* so if we start there and go up to the *A* an octave higher, we've played an *A* minor scale.) Let's just cut to the chase and look at the chords we get when we build chords off of each degree in a minor scale.

Minor Keys

I	ii	III	iv or IV	v or V7	VII	VII7
Cm	Dm	E♭	Fm or F	Gm or G7	A♭	B♭ or B♭7
D♭m	E♭m	E	G♭m or G♭	A♭m or A♭7	A	B or B7
Dm	Em	F	Gm or G	Am or A7	B♭	C or C7
E♭m	Fm	G♭	Abm or A♭	B♭m or B♭7	B	D♭ or D♭7
Em	F♯m	G	Am or A	Bm or B7	C	D or D7
Fm	Gm	A♭	B♭m or B♭	Cm or C7	D♭	E♭ or E♭7
G♭m	A♭m	A	Bm or B	D♭m or D♭7	D	E or E7
Gm	Am	B♭	Cm or C	Dm or D7	E♭	F or F7
A♭m	B♭m	B	D♭m or D♭	E♭m or E♭7	E	G♭ or G♭7
Am	Bm	C	Dm or D	Em or E7	F	G or G7
B♭m	Cm	D♭	E♭m or E♭	Fm or F7	G♭	A♭ or A♭7
Bm	C♯m	D	Em or E	F♯m or F♯7	G	A or A7

Note that in a minor key, we have more options for the types of chords: the IV can be major or minor, as can the V (and we can color these chords in fancier ways too—minor keys have a lot of harmonic ambiguities that we can play with). As in the previous chart, I've highlighted the friendlier keys, with fewer sharps and flats; from a guitarist's point of view, the simplest keys are *Dm, Em,* and *Am.* The i, iv, and v are once again the most common chords, but the other chords in the chart are frequently used as well.

That's just scratching the surface of chord theory, but you can see how useful this kind of information is for helping you zero in on a few chords out of a huge universe of possibilities. Learning the rules is especially advantageous for a songwriter if you also develop your ear for breaking them. Many a great song has been written by following a familiar pattern, then throwing in one fresh and surprising move. Beatles, anyone?

❖ *Chords by the numbers.* Perhaps the most important point you can draw from the above discussion is that chords in a key have a relationship to each other that can be expressed by a number—traditionally, it's a Roman numeral. So if you have a song in the key of *C* that uses *C, F,* and *G* chords, you could say it uses the I, IV, and V. If you train yourself to think of these chords by their numbers rather than by their note names, you will soon see how the same relationships operate in all the keys. For instance, in the key of *G,* a I–IV–V song would use *G, C,* and *D*; in the key of *A,* the I, IV, and V would be *A, D, E.* This understanding is useful in many ways. For example, if you decide that your song in *G* would sound better if pitched a little higher for your voice, you could *transpose* it to the key of *A* by simply finding the I, IV, and V chords in *A* (namely *A, D,* and *E*). And if you discover a very cool chord change in one key, you can figure out how to get the same sound in a different key.

Let's say you just learned a song in the key of *C* that uses this nice move from *C* to *F* to *Em.* Looking at the major-chords chart on page 45, you find that this sequence is I to IV to iii. Armed with this information, you could follow the same pattern in a different key: in *G,* you could play *G* to *C* to *Bm*; in *A,* it would be *A* to *D* to *C♯m.* You have learned the underlying musical logic, not just memorized a particular sequence of chords.

A lot of musicians (especially outside the jazz world) opt to use plain old numbers rather than Roman numerals. This is called the *Nashville number system,* and you might find it a little more user friendly. You add an *m* after the number to indicate a minor chord, a 7 for a seventh chord, and so on, and you can write a quick chord chart like this:

| | | 6m 6m 4 5 | |

Each number represents one measure. That's the chord progression for "Stand by Me" (*A* to *F♯m* to *D* to *E*) and many a '50s rock song. A basic 12-bar blues progression would look like this:

| | | | | 4 4 | | 5 4 | 5

To indicate a chord with an alternate bass note, you use a slash: 1/3 means the 1 chord with the 3 note in the bass (in *G*, that would mean *G/B*).

Thinking of chords by the numbers makes your knowledge of chords and their relationships to each other easily applicable to different keys and different songs. And that is exactly what you are doing as a songwriter: storing away ideas that you hear in other songs and then mixing and matching them to create something new. Number systems also are very efficient for communicating with other musicians, which is why they are the lingua franca for session musicians. You will much more quickly grasp a song that uses *F, B♭,* and *C7* when you understand that these are simply the I, IV, and V7 chords in a key (*F*) you may not play in all that much.

❖ *Progressions and substitutions.* A chord can sound evocative by itself, but its true power lies in how it relates to other chords in a *progression,* or sequence. We've already talked about the most fundamental chord relationship: how the V chord wants to resolve to the I. Songwriters play off that relationship by building tension (delaying the resolution to the I) and finally letting it release (resolving to the I). Let's look at a few other possibilities.

Each major chord has a close cousin known as its *relative minor.* Basic chords are made up of three notes, and a major chord and its relative minor have two of those notes in common. For instance, *C* major is made up of the notes *C, E,* and *G.* Its relative minor, *A* minor, is made up of *A, C,* and *E.* This means that to go from *C* to *Am* in a chord progression is very smooth and natural. Oftentimes, songs use the relative minor relationship to contrast a verse with a chorus: a song in *C* major will sound like it's shifted to the key of *A* minor in the contrasting section. Because the two chords are so close, you can often substitute the relative minor for a major chord (or vice versa) without changing the melody, and give a different flavor to your song. Or if you're writing a song that sits on the *C* chord for a long time—say, four measures—you could try playing two measures of *C* and two of *Am* to keep things moving.

We can identify these relationships on our chords-in-a-key charts: in a major key, vi is the relative minor of I, ii is the relative minor of IV, and iii is the relative minor of V. But in this case it's even more useful to simply commit the chord pairs to memory, because no matter what key you are in, you can try substituting one for the other.

Relative Minors

Major Chord	Relative Minor
C	Am
D♭	B♭m
D	Bm
E♭	Cm
E	C♯m
F	Dm
G♭	E♭m
G	Em
A♭	Fm
A	F♯m
B♭	Gm
B	G♯m

The best way to learn about chord relationships is to let your favorite songs and your ears be your guide. Pick a song with a memorable progression and see how the chords fit into these charts, then write them down by the numbers. Take note of specific chord moves that you find particularly sweet or powerful, and you might find that these moves are "off the chart." The songwriter is giving you something other than what you expect to hear, zigging when you think that the song will zag. Analyze what's going on in these moments, and try applying the same moves to your own songs in progress.

Example off the tip of my fingers: Today I was strumming the Beatles' song "I Should Have Known Better." As in many Lennon and McCartney songs, the progression is quite simple but has a nice twist. The song is in the key of *G*, and the verse alternates between *G* (I) and *D* (V), with an *Em* (vi) and a *C* (IV) thrown in. Standard moves. Then comes a pivotal moment in which the progression goes from *C*, not to *D*, as it has done several times, but to a tasty *B7*, leading to an *Em*. That *B7* is the III7, but our chart says that in a major key, the III is normally minor. Hmm. Also, the section that follows the *B7* sounds like it's shifted into the key of *Em*; if you think of *Em* as the i chord, *B7* is the V7 leading into it—so essentially *B7* is acting as a transition chord between the two keys. So what would that same move be in other keys? In *C*, the III7 is *E7*. In *E*, it's *G#7*—a chord a guitarist like me would be unlikely to reach for. Playing the I into the III7 sounds very ragtimey. . . . This is an idea to stow away and use.

We have been focusing on chord relationships in a key, but we can apply the same kind of thinking to an individual chord. A chord is formed from degrees in a scale (for instance, a major chord is built from the 1, 3, and 5 of the major scale), so with a little music-theory woodshedding you can learn why an *A* minor 6 is called an *A* minor 6, or conversely you can figure out the name of that bizarre but cool chord you just played by accident. And again, the theory allows you to apply that information to other chords and songs. If I had to prioritize theoretical knowledge, though, I'd say that, for songwriting, the way chords fit together in a sequence is much more important than the color of an individual chord; many a weak song has been written by a songwriter captivated with some lush chord—it's so beautiful that he or she forgets to write a real song over it. Songs are defined by motion and the unfolding of time, and that's precisely what progressions are all about.

❖ *Song form.* You can also zoom back and consider the bigger picture: what the sections of a song are and how they fit together.

The simplest song form uses only *verses:* repeating music with changing lyrics that often tell a story, as in a traditional-style ballad (think "Man of Constant Sorrow," "Scarborough Fair," "All Along the Watchtower"). In pop songs, verses typically lead to a *chorus* or *refrain:* the repeating music and words that are the centerpiece of the song ("The answer, my friend, is blowin' in the wind," "So bye-bye Miss American Pie," "Every little thing she does is magic"). As you can see from the last three examples, the chorus often contains the *hook,* which lodges into your head as the word suggests, and the song's title.

Some songs have a *bridge,* also known as the *middle eight,* which offers a musical contrast to both verse and chorus (or just verse, if there's no chorus) and often is played only one time. In "Over the Rainbow," the bridge is the section beginning "Someday I'll wish upon a star"; in "Yesterday," it begins with "Why she had to go"; in "Don't Let Me Be Lonely Tonight," it's "Go away then, damn you."

Verse, chorus, and bridge are the three basic sections most songwriters work with, shuffled around in a million ways. Some songs also include a *prechorus,* which a listener might not really hear as a separate section. The prechorus is a kind of connector between verse and chorus that's intended to build anticipation and make you swoon with pleasure when the chorus arrives; often the lyrics repeat in the prechorus, making it seem like part of the chorus itself. In the Pretenders' "Brass in Pocket," the prechorus begins with "Gonna use my arms"; Tom Petty's "Refugee" has a short prechorus starting with "It don't make no difference to me."

If you map out songs according to their sections, you can think about all the devices the songwriter uses to make them both stand out from each other and work together. These include variations in rhythm (faster, slower, a different groove); melody (often rising higher in the chorus than in the verse, or changing the length and style of its phrases); texture (e.g., sparse accompaniment on the verse leading into a dense chorus and back again); key (modulating to a different tonal center for the bridge or chorus); rhyme scheme (often different in the verse and in the chorus); and language (say, pensive in the verse and defiant in the chorus).

As you think about the form of a song, pay attention to repetitions. When sections repeat, do they repeat exactly, or are there subtle changes going on? Generally, the more a section repeats, the more necessary it is to vary small details within that section (or, if there are lots of verses, to tell a really good story). The chorus, for instance, often evolves through the song, perhaps with variations in the words or embellishments to the melody.

Another aspect of song form, mentioned above, is the structure of the lyrics. How does the rhyme scheme work? (In a four-line verse, do the first and third lines, and the second and fourth lines, rhyme in an ABAB pattern? Or do they rhyme in pairs, like AABB? And does the chorus follow the same pattern as the verse? Do the lines end with exact rhymes (*love* and *above, stand* and *hand*) or near rhymes (*stone* and *home, lay* and *grade*)? Are there internal rhymes in addition to or instead of end-of-line rhymes? Are there specific phrases that repeat within the verses?

In my experience, this kind of lyrical analysis can be interesting to do with a favorite song but is a little too self-conscious and English paper–ish to be productive in the writing process itself. But that's my bias—if you find it illuminating to consider your lyrics in this light as you're working on a song, go for it.

The same goes for the whole topic of music theory and song form. Many artists make up songs with absolutely no awareness that they are stringing together a verse and chorus and bridge, or that they are playing a vi–ii–V–I progression or using an AABA rhyme scheme—they just listen to where the song wants to go. For others, these theoretical tools help to focus and guide the songwriting process. The majority of writers are probably somewhere in between, conscious of some aspects of their craft and completely unconscious about others. Try some of these theoretical approaches and see which ones fit in with your personality as a writer. You may find that they lead you to songs that you would not have written by sheer instinct alone, and that they just generally help you to write more.

THE EDITING PROCESS

Sure, it happens: lightning strikes, and within a miraculously short time you've got a new song. You sputter trying to explain . . . It's like the song writes itself, just appears out of the ether and floats right through your instrument and voice—you almost feel sheepish taking credit for it. And the song is so sure of what it's saying and why it's here—every note and syllable just seems *right*. All you can do is sit back and gaze with admiration at this amazing gift.

Sure, it happens—and hallelujah when it does. But most of the time whole songs don't appear by divine intervention. They arrive piece by piece, over days or weeks or months, or as nominally complete songs that actually consist of a few really good parts and then some filler that basically sets up the good stuff and finally a couple of things that make you cringe. In other words, yup, you've got editing and rewriting ahead. In fact, many songwriters feel that reworking the material that needs it puts you in a position to receive the coveted songs that arrive in finished form.

I think unless you're willing to do your homework on the hard ones, the easy ones don't come.

—Greg Brown

Editing and rewriting require a different mind-set than the one you used to chase down your original inspiration—it may even be helpful to think of the creator and the editor as separate personas. You the creator have an idealized version in your head of what this song is or should be; you the editor respond to the actual notes and words from the perspective of a listener hearing the song for the first time, and you ask the tough questions about whether the song really delivers the goods. Ever practical and even hardheaded, the editor scrutinizes every detail of the song and wonders, is this really necessary? Could this part be stronger, more vivid, more concise? While the creator has all sorts of personal attachments to what has been written, the editor has to be prepared to cut perfectly good stuff, perhaps even great stuff, because it simply doesn't serve the song.

To do this, you need some distance from your creation. When a song inspiration first strikes, you should spill out and record as much stuff as you can *without* filtering too much; that'll give you lots of material to work with later. Then take a break, and come back fresh and ready to be an editor. Record your work-in-progress if you haven't already, and as you listen back, try to imagine that you're hearing and critiquing someone else's work. Which parts really turn you on, and where do you start twiddling your thumbs or thinking about how you need to go grocery shopping?

This isn't always easy to do with your own song, which is why so many songwriters look to co-writers and friends to be sounding boards for their ideas (see below for insights into how the team approach works). But you can learn to be an effective editor, and your songs will surely benefit. The editing process varies from song to song, but here are some ideas about where to look for weak links and how to strengthen them.

❖ *Cut to the chase.* The song form is extremely concise, and you need to grab your audience's ear right from the first note and syllable. Some opening lines are real showstoppers (for instance, John Gorka's "I'm from New Jersey, I don't expect too much / If the world ended today, I would adjust"), but you don't necessarily have to dazzle people with your cleverness. The critical thing is just to start painting the scene, revealing something about the character or the emotion, setting the story in motion. If the opening lines amount basically to throat clearing, and the song's real statement doesn't arrive until verse two or three or the chorus, consider whether that later section might actually work in the beginning. In the writing process, sometimes you need to write preliminary stuff that helps you figure out what you're really trying to say—and then once you've figured that out, you should leave the preliminary stuff behind.

On the musical side, does your song start off strong and distinctive or sound like a thousand other songs? There are certain intros (mid-tempo strumming on the I chord, a standard 4/4 rock drum pattern by itself for a couple measures before the band kicks in) that have been done so many times that they make listeners' minds wander immediately, and you may never get their attention back. Try playing your song without its introduction—just skip right to the first verse—and see if you are really missing anything important. You might be able to take a more interesting chord move or riff from later in the song and use that as the intro, or in some cases you can just lop off much or all of your introduction and get things rolling more quickly.

❖ *Make more from less.* Imagine that you're packing for a trip and you're allowed to bring only one small suitcase. You've got piles of stuff all over the bed that you think might be nice to have along (What if it happens to snow in June? What if I get invited to a black-tie party?), but there's no way it'll all fit. What do you truly *need* to bring? Separating the extraneous from the essential can be hard, but think how great you'll feel traveling so lightly.

So it is in songwriting: your song doesn't have to be short and simple, but every part of it is important and has to contribute to your main idea. And the less clutter you have overall, the more attention people will pay to what remains. This means you have to ask yourself questions such as, Have I taken three verses to say what I could say in one?

> I think it's a great challenge to try to be concise with writing a song. Any songwriter with a certain degree of experience can get an idea across—it may take five verses or whatever. We challenge ourselves to be really concise and really clear in what we're saying. . . . We'll combine verses—we'll take the first two lines of one verse and the last two lines of another. . . . We are not afraid to merge songs together to make one better song: take three different song ideas—what you think are three different songs—and make them one. It's exciting on the quality level and very sad on the quantity level.
>
> —Ed Robertson

The same principles apply to the way you use language within an individual line. When you want to make a scene particularly vivid, it is always tempting to pile on descriptive words, but they start to compete with each other so that the listener doesn't get a clear picture at all. Watch out for mixed metaphors: the love that's "solid as a rock" in one moment and makes you "soar" the next. Trim back to the one adjective or image that really counts: instead of "the blazing, burning fire," just say "the flame." Extend or complement the images you have already used rather than introduce completely new ones. When I am editing words in this way, I picture a tree after a winter storm with its branches bent down nearly to the ground from the snow: I'm taking a shovel and knocking the snow off in clumps, and the limb rises as the weight falls off, eventually springing back to its natural shape.

You have to be economical on the musical side too. Sometimes songs have an extra section that they are better off without, or maybe an instrumental part that sounds cool but is a distraction from the story you're trying to tell. On a micro level, there might be some lag time that you can cut. Take inspiration from the original country blues players, who were not beholden to any 12-bar blues formula. They freely added and dropped beats or measures, changed chords when it felt right, cut a line short here, extended a line there. Go where your song wants to go, when it wants to go there.

Kelly Joe Phelps

❖ *Be specific.* In your lyrics, a specific action or thing or piece of dialogue has so much more power than description, no matter how skillfully it is rendered. You can say that a character is upset, but if he punches through a window pane, we really see it. You can say she left him, but if he's breathing a cloud of exhaust in an empty driveway, we really taste it.

Take a look at these opening lines from Ferron's "Ain't Life a Brook": "I watch you reading a book / I get to thinking our love's a polished stone / You give me a long, drawn look / I know pretty soon you're going to leave our home." We've heard a zillion breakup songs, but in the space of four simple lines Ferron uses just the right details (the book, the loaded look, the stone) to cut to the heart of a disintegrating relationship. You will find this quality in the work of all great lyricists—the meaning of the song is compressed into every detail. Among contemporary songwriters, I highly recommend checking out the work of Gillian Welch and David Rawlings as an example of how much meaning can be packed into very few words and very sparse details.

A friend of mine who is a great songwriter studied poetry in college, and one of her teachers said when you write, you should be able to pick up the page and shake it and have all this stuff fall off of it. Things, you know, shoes, cars, wheelbarrows, windows, cigarettes, ashtrays, whatever—things should be in there. When you put those kinds of things in, it makes a better picture; there's more stuff to grab onto. The message itself might be abstract—you may not even understand in the end what the heck the song is about, but there is a lot of stuff you have taken away and put in your pocket. Whereas with other songs, you can follow it completely, one word after the other, but by the time you get done, it's just a piece of stale bread.

—Kelly Joe Phelps

Notice how he called it "a piece of stale bread" rather than an understandable but forgettable song?

In editing, look for places where you're telling the listener how someone feels or summarizing a story development, and replace those pieces with specific and evocative details. What's the character wearing or drinking or saying? What season is it? What memory is flashing through his or her mind? What smell is in the air?

❖ *Tell a story.* You may not be telling a dramatic or bawdy tale, but as Steven Page of Barenaked Ladies reminds us, the song is a storytelling vehicle, and even mood songs evolve from beginning to end.

> *In a short story you've got essentially what happens in a novel in an incredibly condensed form. There is some sense of change—some kind of an epiphany, or an ending that is uplifting or downturning. You don't know where you're going, but you know that you are on a journey that you trust when you're reading. It's the same thing in a song: you trust in the song to take you somewhere that you may or may not expect.*
>
> —Steven Page

Chances are you do have in mind some kind of movement or change or revelation that happens between your first verse and the final chorus. But the bottom line is, does your listener really get it? You might be projecting things into your song that are not really there or that are just too subtle for anyone but you to notice. Try making your plot line more explicit, and consider whether there are parts of the song that simply don't move the story along. Perhaps cutting some material in the middle would open up the room for you to write an extra verse or two and bring your story to a real climax.

❖ *Use a consistent point of view.* Make sure you haven't inadvertently switched point of view or person in your song—writers sometimes go from *I* to *you* or *she* and back again without even being conscious of it. Think about who is narrating your song and follow that person's perspective throughout, because the same events look different through different eyes. The narrator's language and choice of detail should reveal something of his or her own character even if the story is about someone else. If there is nothing revealing about the narrator's perspective, why is that person telling the story?

Sometimes you can end a songwriting stalemate by changing the point of view or the narrator. For instance, if you are writing in first person, you may feel too obliged to be true to the facts of your

Steven Page of Barenaked Ladies

own experience. Switching the entire song over to *he* or *she* (even temporarily) may free up your imagination to conjure the best story possible, while remaining "true" to the emotions that sparked it in the first place.

> When something rings true, it doesn't even have to be biographically correct. I wrote a song that was a No. 1 hit for Willie Nelson called "There's Nothing I Can Do About It Now." At the time, Willie's whole marriage had blown up and he was getting a divorce, and he was just shifting so many things in his life. He wasn't writing, but he was making this record. . . . The lines of the song are written from a male standpoint: "I see the fire of a woman's scorn turn her heart of gold to steel," all these descriptive kind of Willie Nelson–esque lines. But the feeling of the song, the emotional place of the person singing the song, was really ringing true from my own experience.
>
> You are not limited to an exact replica of what you wrote in your diary. You can go beyond the parameters of your own experience and yet use the emotions that you have experienced. That's what I have become most interested in as a songwriter. It's like I am not doing it alone. It's as if I opened this channel and all this assistance comes through—that sounds very new age, but it is magical. And I end up learning something from my own songs a lot of the time.
>
> —Beth Nielsen Chapman

❖ ***Allow yourself to be simple.*** As counterintuitive as it seems, one of the greatest challenges in songwriting is to be simple—which is not the same thing as being simple minded or simplistic. When a simple, direct expression pops up, singer-songwriters sometimes greet it with skepticism, thinking that this idea must be trite or overused. Shouldn't a song be more crafty or surprising than that? Well, not always. Several artists have told me that songs they initially thought were too obvious turned out to be favorites of their audiences. Those songs are easy to remember and easy to sing and communicate effortlessly, a quality that Pete Seeger admired in the work of his old traveling partner Woody Guthrie.

I tell you, I learned the genius of simplicity. He didn't try to get fancy, he didn't try to show how clever he was, and he was leery of trying a lot of chords. Even songs that literately demanded a double dominant—that is a super tonic—he would not do it. Like "Do Re Mi," he used the tune of a country song, "Hang out the front door key, babe / Hang out the front door key," and if you're playing in G, you should hit an A major 7 there. Woody refused to. He was rebelling against all that cleverness, and he would hit a plain D7.

—Pete Seeger

The most interesting sorts of commercial music are the ones that find an emotion and put it out there. It might not be that subtly done; it might be kind of crude. But when a commercial writer finds an emotion and is able to articulate it in such a way that it's really clear, then everybody gets it and everybody wants to hear it. There's a skill, but it's in the background—it's not the first thing you hear. The first thing you hear is the emotion. . . . I think in the singer-songwriter genre, sometimes the intellect takes over a little too much and everybody gets a little too clever.

—Stephen Fearing

In a song, just as the music can get bogged down by ambitions and self-conscious cleverness, the lyrics can try too hard to be poetic. In reality, songs and poems are very different things. Dense language and complicated constructions might work on the page but sound clunky in a song, blocking the flow of the music.

Songwriting has a very defined structure, and it almost always sounds better when it rhymes or has some sort of internal rhyming. I find that if I take poetry and put it to music, it doesn't work, because it doesn't fit the structure that a song needs—it needs to have four lines pretty much, and a chorus that recurs. Poems don't revolve around that at all.

—Jewel

❖ *Make the melody stand on its own.* One very common weakness is for the melody to be too closely tied to the chord progression (especially if the chords were written first). Play your song chord by chord and see how the melody relates to the chords beneath it. Is the melody note frequently the root note of the chord? Does the melody tend to move when the chords move and stay put when the chords stay put? When you sing the song a cappella, does the melody sound weak? Doubling the melody with the accompaniment part (as in old blues and mountain ballads) can have a powerful effect, but the melody has to run the show.

It's surprisingly easy to lift a melody free from the chord progression, just by moving some parts of it off the dominant chord tones (especially the root) and varying the phrasing. Particularly sweet melodic passages often are the result of the songwriter's stretching beyond the notes that are specifically in the accompanying chords. Lately I've been playing "Singin' in the Rain" in the key of *F*, and the accompaniment basically swings between *F* and *C7* (I and V). While picking out the melody on my guitar, I noticed that the melody keeps falling to a *D*, which is not part of either chord but harmonizes nicely with both (making the *F* sound like an *F6* and the *C7* sound like a *C9*). Much of the character of that melody comes from that one inspired note choice.

❖ *Build contrast between sections.* If you are using a verse/chorus form, the chorus is your moment to stand and deliver a ringing declaration, the words and music you most want your audience to go home singing. So the two sections shouldn't blur together too much: the chorus melody should rise higher than the verse, for instance, or use different phrase lengths and rhythms (see the discussion of song form earlier in this chapter). You might be able to rewrite the chorus melody to make it stand out more, or you might tinker with the chord progression by substituting an individual chord or moving into a different key center.

If the verse/chorus/verse/chorus/verse/chorus form is getting monotonous, you might need to add in a section, perhaps a full-on bridge or an instrumental solo. Even a short break can refresh your listeners' ears and let the most important parts of your song sink in.

❖ *Watch the transitions.* On the other hand, maybe you are trying to join two sections that are *too* different from each other. One tip-off that there's a problem is an awkward or abrupt transition; it sounds like you're driving too fast around a sharp curve. If you have incorporated an old idea that you have always wanted to use in a song, be sure that it really belongs, that you're not just being opportunistic. Great songs have a natural flow; one idea grows out of another and into the next.

When you are adding a new section to a song, try revamping or extending the elements from what you have already written (melody, chords, images) rather than interjecting something completely new. When you build from within like that, your whole song will have a satisfying coherence.

❖ *Check the emphasis.* Joni Mitchell once sang to me three different versions of the line "Since I lost you" (from her song "Man from Mars," which she was in the middle of recording at the time) to show how you can adjust the melody to make the emphasis fall on the most important word (in this case, *lost*), the way we do when we speak. This relationship between the words and the music is sometimes called *prosody.* When the prosody is right on (Mitchell cited Paul McCartney's musical setting of the word *yesterday* as an example), we don't even think about it, because the language just sounds so natural.

When I was getting ready to record my first piece of radio journalism, my editor at NPR made the excellent suggestion that I print out my script, highlight the most important words in each sentence, and then make sure I emphasized those words when I read them aloud. That's a good exercise for lyrics too: write them out, highlight the critical words purely from a reader's perspective, and see if those are the same words that are emphasized in the music. Small adjustments to how you sing a line or structure a verse make a big difference.

❖ *Make sure you're barking up the right tree.* If you have identified a problem line in your song but just can't make any headway in fixing it, you may be focusing on the wrong place: for example, the fact that you can't find a good rhyme in one line might mean that you need to change the previous line that you are trying to rhyme with (did it happen to end with *orange?*). In other words, everything that leads up to a particular line in the song defines your options for what to write there, and if you change the lead-in, your problem may just disappear. It's like tuning a guitar: if the second string seems to be out of tune, there is a good chance that the third string is actually out of tune and making its neighbor sound bad. Once you address the real trouble spot, the second string sounds fine.

I find that an effective way to fix small songwriting problems is to idly think about them while I'm doing something else—driving, jogging, cooking. Several artists have told me they work out solutions while they sleep, which is a neat trick. When you are less focused on the task of songwriting and feeling less pressure, your mind may stumble upon a solution that eluded you when you were sweating it out in front of your notebook and your instrument, or at least you might come up with some new approaches that you can try in your next concentrated song-writing session.

Case in point: I've been working on a song for which I had the complete music and one good verse and then . . . I just couldn't figure out what to write next (why is that second verse always so hard?). Weeks later, a couple of new lines finally popped into my head at the oddest, most preoccupied moment (giving my toddler a bath, if you must know), and later that night I wrote lyrics all the way to the end. Cool! But when I looked back the next day at what I'd written, I found that I liked everything *except* the lines that gave me my breakthrough and that I thought were so good at the time. A month later, I think I've finally got a decent rewrite of those two lines. Moral of the story? You never know— be ready and open for anything at any time.

❖ ***Finally, beware of rules.*** Everywhere you turn, someone will be happy to tell you (or, actually, sell you) the rules of songwriting, the secret behind every No. 1 hit of the last 50 years. But the way in which your song breaks a rule or defies a formula could be its best quality. The goal of editing is not to make your song conform, but to understand what it is trying to say and to do whatever you can to make that statement ring loud and clear. You are spotlighting the strengths and cutting back the weaknesses. Above all, you are listening to where the song wants to go.

The editing process can involve some very rational and pragmatic thinking, but you also need to respect the mysteries and ambiguities inherent in all art. Songs, like life, ripple outward into things that we may feel or sense but not understand. It sounds paradoxical, but you are trying to be very specific in evoking what may be ultimately inexplicable.

It's a good thing to not pretend that you understand everything. You can write a song or sing a song about something and actually leave it saying, "I don't know what this is about." You're singing about your confusion about it, the fact that it's a mystery to you. That's a good thing because that's a true thing. You don't understand everything. When you sing about relationships, I don't know how you can tie it up in the end because so much of it is not understandable.

—Kelly Joe Phelps

COLLABORATING

Opening up your songwriting process to another person might seem like a scary prospect (my baby!), but it can do wonders for your songs. A collaborator might see a problem that needs attention or a solution that has eluded you, suggest approaches that never occurred to you, or simply encourage you to keep chasing down a great idea. There are many levels of collaboration, from asking a friend, "Hey, what do you think of this?" to full-on co-writing. Let's consider a few possibilities.

There's a time in writing by yourself when you lose all perspective on what you're doing—you have two options and you are not sure which one is better; there's a section in the song that drives you nuts, but you just can't figure out how to fix it; you no longer have any idea whether the song is saying what you want it to say or if it's any good at all. The solution? Ask someone you trust—a friend with a good ear, a spouse, another musician, a fellow songwriter, anyone who is sympathetic but is also not afraid to tell it like it is.

I run a song by them and they will make a suggestion—that line doesn't work, or why don't you get rid of that word, or use this word instead of that word, or put that verse up top, that kind of thing. Or sometimes it's just encouragement to keep writing it—"That's worth working on."

I think most songwriters come up at least against questions: What about this line? Is this line better? Or you might really get stuck and need somebody to just show you the door and make you realize that there are a lot more options.

—Louise Taylor

Singer-songwriters who cultivate these kinds of relationships often find that they become indispensable: they streamline the writing process and encourage tighter, more mature songs.

I don't know how people write without an editor. It's so much easier when someone says to you, "Look, that line is not good" or "That's a cliché" or "You can make that better" or "That line really is good." It's incredibly helpful.

—Lucy Kaplansky

A bandmate or performing partner is an obvious candidate for songwriting collaborator. That person already understands and helps shape your music onstage, and collaborating on the writing just gets him or her in on the ground floor. Here's how the Indigo Girls duo described the kind of feedback they give each other during the editing and arranging process.

We'll ask, "What do you think of this?" and the other person might say, "I think the chorus is too long" or "I think we should add a bridge" or "I'm missing this element." If the song's important enough for the person to have written it and believe in it themselves, then you've got to give it a chance.

—Amy Ray

You have to have faith that the process is working. You have to get used to someone else's ideas being added to your song. You're used to just singing it alone and you know the song in an intimate and personal way, and then all of a sudden it's become something else. But I have faith in what Amy and I have done for so

long, and while sometimes it's an adjustment at first, in the end
the song usually comes out being better.

—Emily Saliers

In a band situation, ideas often pop up during rehearsals and jam sessions that the lead songwriter(s) can then shape into real songs. Rob Hotchkiss, for instance, related how his band Train wrote a whole album's worth of material by starting with grooves and riffs improvised (and taped) during sound checks. The band collectively worked the most promising ideas into real song structures, and then frontman Pat Monahan finished them off with melodies and lyrics.

Amy Ray and Emily Saliers—the Indigo Girls

When it's a jam, it can only go so far. It usually stays in E minor, because you can't all switch directions at the same time. So you take one part, and you say, "Great part. We need a prechorus and we need a bridge." Or you say, "If it went to F♯, it would be great right here." And then you work your way toward it.

—Rob Hotchkiss

Co-writing is the most complete form of collaboration: two songwriters meeting on equal ground and bringing their individual talents to bear on a collective creation. You co-write to stretch beyond your own capabilities, complement your strengths with someone else's strengths, and explore styles you couldn't really pull off on your own. This relationship could last for only one song or for an entire career. When a great songwriter discovers his or her musical soulmate, the results can be magical (Rodgers and Hammerstein, Lieber and Stoller, Goffin and King, Lennon and McCartney, Garcia and Hunter . . .).

Singer-songwriters who have worked solo for years are often surprised by what happens when they try co-writing.

It's a little terrifying. I'm fairly insecure, and I think most songwriters are, that maybe the person is going to laugh at your ideas or find them dumb. But with every co-writing experience that I've had, bar none, we came up with a song, and I've pretty much recorded all of them. Now I don't know if that means my filter is too big or that I've just been very lucky.

I had a built-in default snobbery about co-writing, which was, that's what you do when you're running out of steam and just before you make a kid's record. It was really that kind of mentality. I've found it to be so completely the opposite. The true nature of collaboration is the other person's energy and your energy coming together, and at some point in the creative writing process you get so caught up in the excitement of creating something with a sort of a stranger that all the boundaries drop and everybody starts giggling and making cups of tea and papers are all over the desk. I love that. I go home from those sessions and feel like I am twenty foot tall, and I end up writing more material on my own. So it's been nothing but a good thing for me.

—Stephen Fearing

Co-writing is standard practice in the commercial songwriting world, because it is an efficient way to crank out a lot of songs that maintain a high professional standard. The collaborative process also can lead to songs that are less idiosyncratic and personal than what one songwriter might write—and so may be more easily transferable to a recording artist.

I think good co-writing collaborations should be teaching and learning exchanges. I've written 50 songs with Allan Shamblin— well, Alan Shamblin's strong suit as a writer is imagery and very specific painting of pictures. There are not too many people who are better than him at that. When I started writing with him ten years ago, I was not nearly as adept at that as I am now, and he's part of the reason. And hopefully he would say that I taught him something, because I was always musically well versed and good at the big-picture chorus-lyric kind of thing.

You know, co-writing can be both fabulous and awful, depending on who you are doing it with. In order to find the ten or so soulmates that I now have that I write songs with all the time, I've probably written with over 100 people and maybe written only one song with most of them. It doesn't mean that those experiences were terrible; it just means that the magic wasn't quite there or that we just didn't click on a certain level as people. And sometimes your writing styles just don't mesh, even two writers who really admire each other. But I think the only way to find those people you do click with is to try a lot of people.

—Steve Seskin

In a good co-writing relationship, as in a good marriage, both partners are respectful of each other's talents, open and honest with each other, and unconcerned with who takes credit for what. Each one is ready to be a cheerleader if the other is on a roll, or to step in and take the lead if things are stalled. One writer may concentrate on the lyrical side while the other focuses on the music, but the lines between their contributions are often blurry, because they are each giving editorial feedback to the other's ideas. If one person writes almost all the lyrics but the other comes up with the best line, who is the most important lyricist? It's a great song; who cares?

The same philosophy applies to all the sundry ways we have talked about to beg, borrow, steal, coax, tease, and puzzle out your ideas as you are writing a song. If it's a great song, who cares how you got there? All you can do is try a lot of approaches and see what works for you. The measure of your success is right there in the song. Congratulations!

ONSTAGE

Songs these days fly around the world in shiny discs and digital files, yet that dazzling display of technology never changes the fundamental equation of music: a performer, an audience, a song. Just as e-mail doesn't replace a late-night, curled-up-on-the-couch conversation, recordings aren't the same as music communicated person to person.

Performing has a special value for a songwriter. The stage is where you see how your songs fare out in the world: you kiss them good-bye at the bus stop on their way to school, and later they come back to report on who teased them on the playground and who their new friends are. That's not an easy thing for every parent/songwriter to do, but that's how both you and your progeny learn and grow. In writing a song, you have taken your best shot at communicating an idea or story or mood or emotion; putting it out there for an audience is one small test of where you have nailed it and where you haven't quite—not just as a writer, but as an instrumentalist and singer and raconteur. And that test, in combination with all the others conducted in different settings and with different groups of people, helps you set your agenda for improving your existing repertoire and writing the next batch of songs. For a songwriter, there is nothing more validating and thrilling than to witness one of your own creations connecting with a listener.

In the digital age, performing is more important than ever for building an audience and a career. It's fantastic that you can make a CD in your bedroom and post songs on-line, but how do you make anyone outside friends and family notice or care that you did so? The answer, as so many people in the music business will tell you, is still onstage and on the road, making your case audience by audience, song by song. Some artists establish themselves purely through recorded tracks and media promotion, but more often than not, success in the music marketplace is still functionally dependent on your activities down on Mother Earth.

> *Kids come up to me, and they want advice about what's the magic formula to get the national tours and the distribution. You can see they want, want, want all these things. And I think, Maybe you should just try to get a gig. Maybe you should just get a gig, and maybe you should do that every weekend for ten years, and then see if you're not on a haphazard national tour that grew organically and if you don't have some recordings that you made along the way that are distributed through the people you encountered along the way.*
>
> —Ani DiFranco

There are, truth be told, plenty of things about gigging that can just plain suck. The heroic effort made in exchange for barely enough money to buy gas and a cup of watery coffee. The late night followed by the crack-of-dawn start of your day job. The club bookers who never return your calls. The sound guy who butchered your guitar tone. The people gabbing at the front table. The not-all-that-funny-anymore requests for "Stairway" or "Free Bird." The tedium of rental cars and budget motels, the significant others miles away . . . As an emerging artist, you have to develop a thick skin and a long-term perspective, and focus instead on the small things that do go right: the four people who signed your mailing list, the woman who said she loved the last song of the set and wanted it on CD, the couple you recognized from a previous gig.

The circuit of established venues is nowhere near big enough to accommodate all the musicians who could successfully play them given decent promotional support. In some parts of the country and some styles of music, that circuit is basically nonexistent. Fortunately, that situation has inspired music lovers to create viable alternatives—off-the-beaten-track venues where performers might find a small but appreciative audience. The existence of these places means that no matter where you are, you can probably find somewhere to share your songs, either as a first step toward bigger venues or just as a satisfying outlet in and of itself.

Let's take a tour through today's performing scene, from stage craft to venues to gear to booking, and listen to words of wisdom from some well-traveled troubadours.

GETTING READY TO PERFORM

There are people who are born entertainers, gregarious types who love nothing more than putting on a show. But for most of us, it takes time and experience to feel confident as performers— in fact, those attracted to the self-contained creative world of the singer-songwriter tend to be introspective souls who are not at all in their natural element onstage. That's certainly true of me— I've always had to be nudged or pushed to perform, even though I'm secretly eager to do it—and many artists over the years have described to me their battles with stage fright. But even the shyest, most reserved singer-songwriters *can* become effective and even great performers, because they have a secret power: belief in their own songs. If it feels good and natural singing your songs in private, you can learn to tap into that feeling in front of an audience, too.

Success onstage begins with comfort in your own skin and with your own music. In performance, you don't act the same as you do hanging out at home—you are accentuating certain aspects of your personality and suppressing others. But the bottom line is that your identity as a performer is some version of yourself, and it has to come across as authentic to the audience. Even if you are taking a more theatrical approach and essentially inventing a stage persona, as David Bowie or Beck does, the character that you are inhabiting has to be someone you (like a good actor) can relate to and deliver with authenticity—just as when you're writing a song in character, you have to identify with that character for the song to come alive.

Louise Taylor once described the realization that helped her overcome her deep discomfort with making music in public.

> It feels good now. It feels like I've come to who I am. I didn't understand that that's what an audience really wants. For a long time I thought they wanted something I imagined you had to be or you had to do, and very slowly I came around to the idea that really what the audience wants you to be is yourself—something that comes across as real.
>
> —Louise Taylor

Nothing teaches you about performing more effectively and quickly than just doing it. You don't have to learn in front of a highly critical audience, either. There are many informal and supportive settings that can help you find your footing before you play on an actual stage (see the next section for ideas), and even when you do make that step, the indifferent audiences you are likely to encounter at first give you plenty of time and space to grow. So cut yourself some slack and consider each show another installment of Gigging 101.

As with songwriting, there are no rules about how to perform successfully—you have to find a style of presentation that suits your personality, your music, your audience, and the venue. Here are some suggestions and observations on stage craft that might help you along the way.

❖ *Practice realistically.* The best way to prepare for any kind of show is to simulate as closely as possible how you will be playing. That means if you plan to stand onstage, practice that way at home. Set up microphones or an amp or whatever you're going to be using, so that you are accustomed to working with your gear. And go through your set from start to finish without taking a break for chips and salsa or tuning up for ten minutes. When you make a mistake, pretend that there is an audience waiting for you to get on with it (more on that below). If you can assemble a small test audience—your friend, spouse, sibling, cat—all the better.

❖ *Practice talking.* You may feel a little silly doing it at home alone, but you can practice the talking as well as the playing. Musicians who are really good at rapping with the audience seem like they are being completely spontaneous, but in reality they are drawing on a repertoire of jokes, stories, and asides that they have developed over a long stretch of gigs. It's just like improvising on an instrument; you are spontaneously recombining and extending all the little riffs and moves you've memorized over the years.

So think in advance about some things you might say during your set. If you are intimidated by the prospect of talking onstage, think small—don't expect or try to become a stand-up comedian overnight. Practice these little raps along with your songs at home, and then at the gig take note of what worked and what didn't, and store that information away for future use. It's a gradual process, finding a way of speaking that fits with your stage persona and your music. Many top-flight entertainers started out anxious and tongue-tied onstage.

When I started I didn't look up from the guitar neck, and I had to write out what I was going to say in between songs, even if it was "This next song's called ..."

—Patty Larkin

My dad was really good at it. He was always the one who would tell stories and make up songs on the spot about audience members. We'd do the four hour-long sets, and we would walk around between sets and talk to everyone. I was really shy and stiff onstage, real self-conscious. And then I went through other phases where I'd been onstage so long, at age 14 or 15, that it would get way too comfortable—you're too relaxed and you don't have any respect for it. You're not entertaining; you're just like in your living room.

I think when I started playing my own music, I came into my own, because I get lost in the emotion of the song—I don't have to think about it at all. I just learned to have a rapport with the audience and talk and tell stories and joke around, and I began to enjoy that as much as singing.

—Jewel

❖ *Use your nerves.* Most people consider the jitters they feel before going onstage to be an obstacle (I'm so nervous, how am I ever going to pull this off?) or a sign of inexperience (if I really knew what I was doing, I wouldn't be so nervous). But there's another way to look at those butterflies in the pit of your stomach: as a source of energy. Nervous energy is what helps you rise above your everyday self and deliver a great show. I have on many occasions chatted with performers both before and after a gig, and I'm amazed at how edgy even the most seasoned and seemingly natural performers are beforehand, and how they are almost like different people when they finally relax afterward. The fact that they still feel that edge before their umpteenth gig is one reason they are so good at what they do.

So think of your preshow nervousness as something that helps you get pumped up to play your best. And remember that the stage is a dynamic environment with a constant energy flow between you and your audience. Your nerves help to generate the musical energy that you send out into the room, and the audience reaction—which is what you are most nervous about—completes the cycle. Even strangers and just-happened-to-be-there listeners want you to succeed, for their own selfish reasons: they want to have a good time. You are in this together.

❖ *Lighten up.* Your songs may be brooding and dark, but that doesn't mean you have to be that way during your whole set. A little self-deprecating joke or aside gives your listeners a necessary breather (there's a reason gallows humor exists) and shows that you don't take yourself too seriously. And lightening up for a moment may in fact heighten the impact of your next sad song.

❖ *Ease into it.* Kick off a performance with songs that are familiar and easy to play and help you get into the groove. Even if you have warmed up well beforehand (which you should do, both your voice and your hands), you need to settle in once your show starts, and so does your audience. If someone is mixing your sound, there's a good chance that he or she will be tweaking the mixing board during your first song, because a room with people in it sounds different from the empty room where you conducted your sound check. So save your tricky stuff and new stuff for later in the set.

❖ *Prepare to be flexible.* A good set list offers well-thought-out variety in mood, tempo, key, and song length, but ideally you should be open to making on-the-spot adjustments. If you keep a few songs in reserve, perhaps jotted down to jog your memory, you'll be ready if you're asked to extend your set beyond what you were originally planning to play (if that happens, congratulations!) or—a more likely scenario—if you want to make substitutions based on how the set is going. If the crowd is not attentive, you might want to skip that subtle mood song and substitute something more direct and upbeat. Or people may respond with surprising enthusiasm to the oddball cover you sometimes play, so maybe it would be a good idea to throw in another along the same lines.

It all boils down to being a listener as well as a player onstage, paying attention to what is going on in the room and with your songs.

> My approach to writing and to performing is I never think of the songs as being done. I don't have in my head a standard version of how this song goes. To me, anyway, they are more alive than that. They tend to want to go off in different directions, and I go with them.
>
> —Greg Brown

❖ *Cater your music to the setting.* The stage is a very different environment from the studio, and savvy performers exploit those differences.

> I see them as quite separate entities and chances to do very different things with your music. There's a kind of energy you can put into that show that you can't do on a record—namely visuals. Just jumping up in the air and moving around and that kind of physical, visual energy adds so much to what you're doing, and you can't do that on a record. We do a lot of improv when we play live,

making up songs and kind of hacking around, that wouldn't stand up with repeated listening. That's not what it's for. It's about the moment, about feeding off the audience, and it might not make sense to a person sitting there listening to a recording of it two months later who's not in the building, who's doesn't know what happened just before it. And similarly, on a record you can do things that are so subtle and so thought out that they would be lost in an arena or a stadium. What we strive to do is to take advantage of both those things.

—Ed Robertson

Not only do you need to adapt your presentation to the live setting, you need to consider which songs are the best choices for your set list. There are songs (originals and covers) that would

Ed Robertson of Barenaked Ladies

seem goofy on a record but are big winners onstage, as well as strong album tracks that somehow don't translate into perform-ance pieces. Just keep trying things and see what works, and over time you will wind up with a live repertoire that overlaps but doesn't precisely match your CD track lists.

❖ *Don't apologize.* So often I have heard novice performers apol-ogize to the audience about the cold they have, their lack of finesse on their instrument, the likelihood they are going to make a mis-take in the new song they are about to play . . . From the audi-ence's perspective, these apologies are simply annoying—you're telling them in advance that you're not going to deliver as good a show as you should or could. Who wants to be told that? Just con-centrate on doing your best given all the limitations and circum-stances of that particular night. If you want to briefly explain that you're recovering from bronchitis and just getting your voice back, that's fine, but don't apologize for the fact that you have been sick. The audience will sympathize and root for you as you give it your best shot.

❖ *Use your mistakes.* Everybody flubs a line or a chord some-times, and it is not a disaster. It's not like stumbling on your triple axel in Olympic figure skating competition, where you know that row of scowling judges just knocked your scores way down and you blew your chance for a medal. On the contrary, a mistake onstage can be an opportunity to bond with your audience if you laugh or shrug it off or play with it. The best performers transform mistakes into great moments: I've heard Martin Sexton, for instance, stop after a garbled line and do a dead-on imitation of a tape rewinding, completely cracking up the crowd. Your audience does not expect you to be superhuman and technically perfect, which is a pretty meaningless concept when it comes to music anyway.

You can prepare yourself to deal with the inevitable glitches. As you practice your set at home, pretend you are in front of an audience and need to make an entertaining or at least smooth recovery from a mistake. Learn how to keep cruising past a small flub, which an audience will soon forget anyway. If it's a bigger mistake, like starting a song in the wrong key or singing the wrong first line of a verse, think about ways to acknowledge the mistake in a light-hearted way and then restart. If you mess up somewhere in the middle of a song, keep the rhythm going while you loop around to make the second attempt, so that you do not completely stop the flow. If you play guitar onstage, be ready to deal with the gremlins of out-of-tune and broken strings. Tuning and string-changing jokes are an entire subgenre of stage humor. I will always remember a fiery festival performance by the late Michael Hedges in which he broke a string and then pulled a spare out of a bag with an exaggerated sweep of his arm, as if he were a knight brandishing his sword for a duel. It was funny and dramatic—who knew grabbing an extra string could be a grandiloquent gesture?— and the crowd loved it.

There's something about walking onstage that makes you think you've got to be good, you'd better not be a disappointment, and you'd better not make a mistake. All of that is horseshit. None of it applies. The opposite is true: you will be a disappointment; you will make mistakes; you will have nights that are just empty at best. And be happy with them.

There's something automatically there when you walk on, by contract. It's what "in concert" means. I think it starts before anybody is in the building. It's something about people knowing that they're going to meet as strangers or otherwise in a room and share this musical experience. You walk out and the motor's running, and what you do is just follow that. That's what's doing the work. It's really delusional to think you are what's happening, because you're not. You are kind of the excuse, maybe the focal point, or more accurately maybe the trigger. What's really going on is just that curve, and if you pay attention to that, boy, it's the most fun on earth.

—Leo Kottke

❖ ***Respect the audience.*** Let's face it: people who are sitting and listening to you play music on any given night have plenty of other things they could be doing. They're giving you their time and perhaps their money, and you need to respect that. You are offering them the gift of your music, but no one appreciates a gift that's sullenly dropped at their feet.

I think I used to feel angry at the audience for looking at me, because I was very shy and not very comfortable with myself. And I've learned that you can't do that; if someone is looking at you, if they've paid money to see you, then you'd better put on a show and not sit there and be morose.

—Suzanne Vega

Respecting the audience doesn't mean you have to be all saccharine smiles and gee-whiz appreciation. There's a long tradition of taking a provocative or confrontational stance with the audience, and that can be very effective in the right setting. But even being aggressive is a form of respecting the audience: it's an acknowledgment that you need to do more sometimes than just play the song, a way of pushing people and starting the cycle of action and reaction that drives a great show.

At times you will encounter audience members who are unforgivably rude, interrupting you or otherwise spoiling the atmosphere. It's never easy, but try not to take these things personally. Rise above it. You have more important things to do than spar with some schmuck who's trying to get attention. Ignoring him might be the best way to silence him anyway.

You can play with a 104-degree fever and your heart fibrillating, but you can't play if you are infuriated. If something is really blowing your stack, you've got to drop that as quickly as possible, because that's the one emotion that can screw it all up for you.

—Leo Kottke

❖ *Acknowledge where you are.* Audiences like to have the feeling that they are part of a unique evening and not just watching a performer do the same show she did last night and the night before and 50 nights before that. Think about ways in which you

Leo Kottke

can acknowledge that you are standing on that particular stage in that particular town on that particular night. It doesn't have to be pumping your arms and shouting, "How ya doin', Schwenksville!" It could be as small a thing as thanking the headliner or sound guy or mentioning someplace you went earlier that day. Such day-in-the-life details are part of the reason why people are there listening to you rather than spinning CDs at home.

❖ *Show them in.* Playing original songs for people who don't know them is a challenging gig. It requires a lot more of your audience than if you were singing pop covers or pounding out formulaic bar-band blues. So think about how you can draw people into the world of your songs. Imagine that your song is a new friend from out of town, and you are bringing him to a party and introducing him around. What might you say? Maybe something about how he grew up on a llama ranch, or about his job as a food stylist, or about how you two met while chaining yourself to a redwood tree in California—whatever you think will be an intriguing detail that will lead to further conversation. Your song introductions can perform a similar function. You don't want to bore people with too much trivia, but a well-chosen anecdote can help them get to know you and your songs a little bit better.

And even if your focus is on original songs, don't rule out playing covers, by the way, especially if you can find a unique slant on a familiar song that makes it feel like yours. In your set, a cover gives listeners a break from the new and unfamiliar and freshens their ears for the next original song. Plus, your taste in covers reveals something about where you are coming from musically and in turn helps illuminate why you write the kinds of songs you write.

❖ *Stay in the pocket.* Performing is an adrenaline rush, and that can easily lead to breakneck tempos. It's thrilling to go fast and feel the wind in your hair, but be careful not to kick off a song at an unsustainable tempo or accelerate to the point that you can't sing the words or play the riff properly. Before you start, hear the ideal groove in your head for a few seconds so you nail it right from the downbeat.

❖ **Work the mic.** Back in high school, I remember listening back to soundboard tapes of my band and wondering for a few disorienting moments who the hell that singer was with the froggy voice. Yup, it was me—I was so amped up by being onstage in front of all those dancing classmates that my voice kept rising into this half yell that completely changed its timbre in a pretty unflattering way. In other words, I wasn't making good use of the microphone pointed at my mouth.

For a singer, a microphone is a great thing: it allows you to whisper and shout and all points in between. So use the mic; it's your friend. And don't be afraid to get right on it, which boosts the low end in your voice and makes you sound big even when you bring it down to a soft hum.

❖ **Use dynamics.** In a setting where you are competing for people's attention, dynamics are one of your best tools. Contrast is the key. Build to a loud climax and then stop abruptly. Do a live fadeout. And if the chatter is starting to drown you out, try bringing your volume way down rather than up. People have become so used to shouted conversations in the back of rock clubs that they are unlikely to surrender if you try to be louder than they are.

When you turn down, it seems that people listen harder. A lot of people's volume approach is to turn the electric guitar up to 12 and people won't be able to help but listen, but our approach has kind of been the softer we are, the more acoustic we are, people will lean in and listen a little bit more.

—Laura Love

❖ *Vary the accompaniment.* When you are performing solo, your voice and your words may be the focus of attention, but your instrument is a lot of what the audience will be hearing that night. So (as we discussed in the last chapter) work hard on giving your songs distinctive and varied accompaniment parts.

You can accomplish this goal without becoming a virtuoso player. If you're a guitar strummer, learn to fingerpick a little. Switch instruments for a song or two; all you really have to know how to do on the other instrument is play that song or two. Sing over hand percussion or a cappella—the unaccompanied voice is always arresting. These kinds of change-ups are so refreshing in the middle of a long stream of songs played on the same instrument.

❖ *Get your gear in order.* We will cover this subject in more detail below, but the last thing you want during a performance is to be worrying about your gear. Keep it simple and functional and as close to trouble free as you can manage. Use your gear at home so there are no nasty surprises at the gig. If you will be using a house sound system, microphone, and other equipment, be sure you know exactly what will be available and that your own gear will be compatible with it. Develop a routine for setting up everything you need (or might need) and then tuning your instruments, and follow it religiously before every show.

❖ *Work with your hosts.* The people who book shows, tend bar, wait tables, run sound, work the door, and handle other roles at the venue won't always treat you as cordially and respectfully as you would hope. But the fact is, they are hosting you. You are providing a service to them, and they are providing a service to you. All of your jobs are a lot of work for not a lot of pay. So no matter how you feel you are being (mis)treated, be a pro: Show up on time, be friendly with your hosts and any other musicians on the bill, and (yes, this is your mother speaking) say please and thank you. Not only will this make your evening more pleasant, but it might win over some allies and lead to more gigs there or elsewhere down the road.

❖ *Build your list.* At every gig, no matter how small, have a place where an interested listener can sign up on a mailing list. Even if you use only e-mail promotion, be sure you get their physical address so you can target your announcements to those who live near where you're playing (no sense telling the folks in Tampa about your gig in Buffalo). A good mailing list is the single most important promotional tool for an independent artist.

If you've got CDs to sell, you should have at least a few on hand. Going home with your disc might make the difference between "Oh yeah, that woman was good—what was her name again?" and a diehard fan, and many performers make a lot more at the CD table than they do from the door. Flyers that announce upcoming events and point people to your Web site are a good idea too. You may not need all this stuff each time, but it's a lost opportunity if someone asks about your CDs and all you can give them is a Web address scribbled on a napkin.

❖ *Take the long view.* If there's a common theme to all this advice, it is to be patient. As much as we all dream about the rocket ride to the stars, most long-term careers in music are built one fan at a time. It takes time to find your groove as a performer and to find the people who respond to what you have to say. No single gig is definitive; each is a step in an ongoing process of developing and learning and sharing.

Remember, too, that there are many varieties of performing musicians. There are those with day jobs who long to devote their lives to music and those who perform occasionally without any professional aspirations. There are the local heroes who teach and gig only in their hometown, the regional acts who stay within a radius of a few hundred miles, and those seemingly full-time pros who tour nationally but actually pay their bills with temp work during stints at home. No matter how you make a living, don't confuse the financial status of your music with its inherent value as art. The moment you get up in front of people to play music, it doesn't matter if you've spent your day doing data entry or teaching fifth graders or polishing your Grammy awards: what counts is the passion and sweat you put into your songs.

And whatever your disappointments and successes in the performing world, remember that when you step onstage and play your songs, you are offering something that no one else can offer: your music and a view of the world from where you (and only you) stand. That is a priceless gift.

FINDING VENUES

In the performing scene today, much more is going on than meets the eye when you flip through the entertainment pages of your local paper. There are the established venues, from arenas on down through theaters and clubs and coffeehouses, but if you dig a little deeper you will also find musical happenings in living rooms, church basements, music stores, and many other unexpected places. For a developing artist, these informal settings are an excellent place to get some experience in front of a sympathetic audience.

Before you even step onto something resembling a stage, though, you can find opportunities for sharing your songs. Start right at your own house—just ask friends or family if they'd like to hear a new song or two. If you feel awkward making the suggestion, drop a large hint by leaving your instrument out in the living room. If you know some local musicians, organize a jam session (collective playing on familiar songs) or a song circle (swapping original and off-the-beaten-track songs). Keep an ear out for these kinds of gatherings in your community. Aside from private parties, such get-togethers might be organized through a local folk society, music store, or church. In warm weather, they may happen at the farmers' market or street fair. Ask around—you might be surprised at what goes on right under your nose.

Summer festivals are a fantastic place to play as well as listen to music. Festivals with a lot of campers often have jam sessions that extend through the night, and at some events (like the Kerrville Folk Festival in Texas) the campfire scene rivals the main stage as an attraction. Each circle tends to have a particular orientation: fiddle tunes, Grateful Dead songs, blues and swing, originals . . . Grab your instrument and scout around for a gathering that best suits what you do, then find a place in the circle. Remember that sharing is a two-way street, though. It's obnoxious to cut in so you can play your song as soon as possible and then take off to find your next slot. Listen and learn. Join in if it seems appropriate, but let each player have his or her moment.

When it comes to locating actual performance venues, the Web is an invaluable tool. Look up the itineraries of artists who do something similar to what you do or are aspiring to do; use either their Web sites or a site that collects concert listings into a database and allows you to search by name, style, location, venue, and so on (see Resources for specifics). You will quickly see that on the lower rungs of the music-business ladder, active performers are playing at all kinds of places other than clubs and coffeehouses. Such as . . .

❖ *Open mics.* Open mics fill an important role as places where anyone can get up and play a song or two on a real stage, sound system and all. Playing at an open mic is worthwhile not just for logging stage time but for making connections with your local music community, since most of the audience consists of other musicians. Many artists have started this way, building from open mics to pass-the-hat sets to actual paying gigs, and even experienced pros show up at open mics to test out new material or just because they want to *play*. When I first moved to the San Francisco area from the East Coast, open mics helped me get my bearings and meet other musicians (including some established performers who hosted these events) and led to a regular gig at one club. In the early '90s, the open-mic scene was where Train first got rolling while several of its members were recovering from a disastrous trip through the major-label system.

We would literally play in front of five people a night. But you know, we would play in front of five people, and one of them would say, "Man, you guys are going to make it," and that would mean something.

—Rob Hotchkiss

Many coffeehouses and clubs host open mics, usually on a slow night early in the week. Some are specifically designed as songwriter showcases, and they might include feedback on your presentation and material. I've participated in members-only open mics organized by the West Coast Songwriters Association, for instance, that include written and oral feedback from guest judges. The open mics and writers' nights hosted by Nashville's tiny Bluebird Café have made it a mecca for songwriters.

The sign-up routines for open mics vary from place to place. Plenty of patience is required, because there's often a lottery in which you show up early to pick a time slot that may end up being many hours later. If you hope that your fellow performers are going to hang around and listen to you, then hang around and listen to them as well—an educational experience in its own right.

You learn a lot more from seeing open mics than you do from seeing polished shows. You just watch what works and what doesn't.

—David Wilcox

❖ ***Bookstores.*** The growth of bookstore chains like Borders and Barnes and Noble, with their large music sections and cafés, has created an entirely new circuit of venues for live music. Big stores may feature some nationally known acts, but they rely on local and developing artists to keep the music flowing week after week. The audience generally consists of people who happen to be there that night, browsing books or sipping lattés, so they may or may not pay attention to you. But then again, people who are out shopping for books and CDs are more likely to be receptive to new music than the average Joe and Jane, so this is a cut above playing at a restaurant or the like.

To look into performing at your local bookstore, stop in during a show and ask who's in charge of booking, then follow up in person or by phone and submit your promo package (see the booking section below). Some stores host open mic nights, which are a good chance to scope out the scene and perhaps to be heard by the event manager. Keep in mind that bookstores are trying to create a stimulating but basically peaceful environment, so save your sonic assaults for a different gig.

❖ ***Music stores.*** Another retail space that is sometimes converted into a performance space is the music store—move those racks of sheet music and guitars out of the way, set up a PA and some chairs, and voilà. This is more likely to happen at a larger shop that doubles as a community music center, with classes, clinics, and jam sessions complementing the retail and repair business. Performances at a music store are often an offshoot of the educational program, featuring regular teachers or visiting clinicians who are sponsored by a manufacturer or publisher. Stop in and find out what's going on at your local music emporium.

Even for musicians not interested in developing a full teaching practice, by the way, it's a big asset to be able to conduct workshops on the side (instrumental technique, stage craft, songwriting, whatever your strength). Workshops help fill in spaces during tours, give you something fruitful to do in the afternoons, and open the door to concert appearances. In the summertime, many road warriors enjoy teaching for a week or two at one of the scores of music camps that happen all across the country, where kids and grown-ups alike come to live and breathe music all hours of the day. An increasing number of these camps offer programs for song-writers, with classes and critiques led by active troubadours.

❖ *Schools.* Since becoming a dad, I have had a blast taking my guitar into preschools and elementary schools to sing songs for and with kids. Kids (especially young ones) are about as respon-sive an audience as you'll ever get: when they like something, they beam and clap and groove, and when they're bored, they fidget and look around for something more interesting to do. They learn songs amazingly fast, and they teach some valuable lessons about songwriting—especially the power of simple expression and the singable melody. They also can be very easily brought into the songwriting process, and making up a song in collaboration with kids (from a familiar melody or from scratch) is an educational and entertaining experience all around.

If you are looking to volunteer your services in a school, all you really have to do is ask—teachers welcome the opportunity to bring special activities like this into the classroom. Paid perform-ances are set up either by an individual school (arranged by a teacher, administrator, or the PTA) or through a central agency; call the school to find out how it works. Compared to regular ven-ues, said veteran school performer Walkin' Jim Stoltz, school gigs are "much more laid back. I don't have to worry about the pro-motion, and booking is generally much, much easier. Folks will return your calls from a school." You will probably have to bring your own equipment to a formal performance, because the gym-nasium isn't, after all, a concert hall.

I think it is very important that performers want to be there for motives beyond money. You have to like kids and enjoy being around them. And you need to have a show that is educational in some way. Most schools want more than just music. They want a theme to the performance that is going to enhance the educational experience of their students. My show has simple environmental lessons but also has ties to science, geography, music, and writing. A teacher can easily use my show to build on a number of subjects and lessons.

My advice to any musicians looking into doing school concerts is to have fun. Teach, but have fun. Talk to the kids as you would to anyone. Don't talk down to them. Keep them involved with what you are doing. Let them participate in the show. Every song I perform is a sing-along, squeak-along, or howl-along. Tell them stories about yourself. The sooner they get to know you, the more successful you will be in getting your message across. Try to have a question-and-answer time after the show with some of the classes. Again, the kids will get to know you better and appreciate what you do much more. When the kids appreciate you, the teachers do too.

—Walkin' Jim Stoltz

❖ *Busking.* Then there is always the sidewalk, the subway station, the pedestrian mall, or the public square—playing for tips in a kind of performance boot-camp environment. Busking is not for shrinking violets, but it can be lucrative and very good for your chops. Peter Mulvey, who forged his style on the streets of Dublin and the subway stations of Boston (and later recorded a CD on his customary subway bench), cited a number of benefits of busking aside from the change collected: It focuses you on the essentials— the melody and the groove. Since nobody is going to pretend to be interested in what you're doing, it provides tangible and immediate feedback; if you reach somebody (and they reach for their wallet), that's a real achievement. Busking is a good way to build a mailing list of locals who might never hear you otherwise. And if you combine daytime busking with evening gigs, when you reach the stage you are warmed up and, in Mulvey's words, "humming like a cable."

> *Just by repetition, eventually you come to those peak moments when you really break through the ice and you are underwater— you're in the song. Whatever the tools you are using, that's the target you're shooting for in performance. And the subway was the first place I learned to do it. Some of the tools that you use in the subway are spontaneity and, actually, frustration. The trains coming and ruining your takes or taking away your audience—it wears you down to a point of surrender, and sometimes that point of surrender gets you into the song. In a bizarre way, sometimes being locked out of it gets you into it.*
>
> —Peter Mulvey

If you think that busking might be for you, you've got to do a little preparation before hitting the street. You probably need a permit, which you get from the town/city for free or a small fee, and you need to suss out local regulations about where, what, and how you can play. Unless you can cut through the ambient noise unplugged, you will have to assemble some sort of portable amplification rig (microphone, battery-powered amp, etc.). And, of course, you have to adapt your repertoire to the rough-and-tumble setting, focusing on songs that will carry over the din of horns and trains and cell-phone conversations. That might mean playing a lot more covers that you normally do, which is, in my view, healthy for a singer-songwriter. Performing great songs by other people is like taking a master class in song craft.

❖ *House concerts.* For grassroots artists and listeners alike, house concerts are one of the brightest opportunities on the performing scene. Filling the voids left by commercial venues, house concerts are hosted by music fans who turn their living rooms or barns or whatever spaces into temporary concert halls. House concerts are like a cross between a private party and a public event: the shows are typically publicized through friends and friends of friends, with limited seating by advance reservation only and an informally collected "suggested donation" that goes mostly or entirely to the performer. Except for the larger and more established house concert series, there's no sound system or stage (in fact, be careful you don't stomp on the toes of people in the front row), and people often bring their own chairs or food to share at intermission. So it's a literally homey event, with very close contact between performer and audience as well as between performer and host, who may offer the guest room and a meal as part of the package.

I've hosted occasional house concerts for several years, and they have some qualities unlike any other shows. For one, the audience

Peter Mulvey

may know little or nothing about the performer or even the style of music that they're going to hear—they are coming because they know the host or their friends invited them or just because the concept is novel and intriguing. Yet they are most definitely there to listen, and you could hear a pin drop in the room. So this is an opportunity to reach listeners who never set foot in clubs but are excited by the prospect of discovering good music in a unique setting. In many ways, it's an ideal situation for a singer-songwriter: for once, nobody is expecting you to supply background music or play their old sing-along favorites.

In this up-close-and-personal environment, talking with the audience during and after your sets is expected and essential. It would seem very strange to just sit there and play your songs. This kind of intimacy may be a little unnerving if you're used to the accompaniment of clinking silverware and murmuring conversations; chatting with people before you play may help break the ice.

The financial arrangements for house concerts vary, but they are often a sweet deal for the artist compared to playing at a club: you get a much higher percentage (or all) of the proceeds, plus CD sales and perhaps free room and board for a night. So you might carry away more money from playing a house concert for 25 people than you would playing for three times that many people in a club, and the host probably did all the legwork of publicizing the show. Unlike clubs that present show after show, week after week, a house concert is a special event for the host and will be treated as such.

These days, house concerts happen all over the country and have become like an underground circuit, especially in the folk world. The Web is the best place to locate existing series and learn more about how house concerts operate (see Resources), but keep in mind that *any* fan with a decent-sized living room is a potential host. (You could suggest that possibility the next time someone comes up and says, "Why don't you ever play in my town?" I did my first house concert with two weeks' notice, responding to an e-mail from a singer-songwriter trying to fill in a last-minute cancellation on her tour.) As you look into playing house concerts, remember that the hosts are volunteering their time and their homes because they love the music; this is not "just business" to them. Although you want to be clear about the arrangement, you should treat your hosts a little differently than you would the presenters at a commercial venue. You might, for instance, normally ask for a guarantee of X dollars, but you shouldn't expect house concert hosts to make that commitment—they're already buying food and drinks as well as setting up and cleaning up, borrowing or renting chairs, and spending a lot of time e-mailing and calling people. Chances are, the host is going to work very hard to fill the room and create a successful evening all around.

❖ *Opening slots.* Opening someone else's show is both a tremendous opportunity and a daunting challenge. You are in a high-profile club, with a crisp sound system and a real backstage. The room is packed and eager . . . for the headliner to play. From the point of view of the club, the opener's job is to warm up the crowd and extend the entertainment beyond the main attraction. From the opener's point of view, this is a chance to step up to the mic and make an impression on a roomful of strangers. On the one hand, there's less pressure on the opener because it is really the headliner's night; on the other, there's more pressure because it is someone else's crowd. "Headliners must fill our niche and have the potential to fill the room," said Griff Luneberg, who books Austin's Cactus Café. "Opening acts only need to be talented."

The reason to pursue opening slots is not for the money, which is minimal, but for the exposure. You are supporting the headliner in order to support your own efforts to be the headliner on a different night. That means, according to Jim Fleming of the booking agency Fleming and Associates, you should always have a follow-up plan: a gig of your own within the next three or four months in the same city (preferably announced by flyers at the CD table), so anyone pleasantly surprised by your opening set can come and experience your full show. That's how you turn the interested listener into a fan.

> *Some performers who open shows feel like they want to show all the variety of what they do, and that's not necessarily the place to do it. If you're playing for only 20 or 30 minutes, you should just go out and knock their socks off, because what you want them to do is remember you. It's not the time to do three ballads or show off your fancy musicianship. Do the rest of it later, when you get your 45 minutes or an hour or two sets.*
>
> —Jim Fleming

> *As a performer, you need to play these types of shows to learn how to play a big room. How does your show translate from 30 people to 3,000? There are differences, and you have to try it a couple times to get the hang of it. The first times I played in front of fanatical audiences, I worried, "Is my sound big enough? Can I hold their attention?" I came to the conclusion that if my songs and the way I performed them solo couldn't make a room of music fanatics be quiet and listen, I was in the wrong business. Nine times out of ten this has worked for me.*
>
> *Most of the time these big shows allow you to meet and spend time with an artist who in many ways is your peer but has more experience and draws a hell of a lot more. There aren't too many ways in the modern music business to have a real mentor relationship; opening shows is one of the few.*
>
> —Erin McKeown

In this supporting role, your professionalism is extremely important. Show up on time, be courteous to the headliner and the people at the venue, keep a low profile, and above all, don't play longer than you're supposed to.

For opening acts, the cardinal sin is going over your allotted time. If it's 30 or 40 minutes, be sure you do not go over. Headliners hate it, club bookers hate it, and you may not get booked again. Remember the audience did not pay to see you. Keep it short and sweet.

—Griff Luneberg

If at the end of your opening set the crowd is dying to hear more, congrats—you have done a bang-up job. Now go out and schmooze with your new admirers, and encourage them to take home your CD and come see you at the coffeehouse next month.

Opening slots are booked in different ways. Often the promoter suggests an opening act but needs approval from the headliner, so in this case, a relationship with the venue is what lands the gig. A headliner might request a specific opening act or bring him/her along on the road, but this is relatively rare in the singer-songwriter world outside of big names and big halls. Since the headliner is always involved one way or another in the selection of the opening act, networking with other, compatible artists helps to bring these gigs your way.

It is possible to focus too much on openers and not enough on your own shows. At some point, Jim Fleming said, it's better to play your own show for 200 people than it is to serenade 2,000 people while they are buying beer and taking their seats for the main attraction. Look at openers as a way to poke your head into a higher level of the music business than where you are currently standing. With time and work, you may get to that place where yours is the big name on the marquee and someone else is supporting you.

Gear Matters

My whole life is the way that guitar sounds coming back through the monitors.

—Ani DiFranco

There are basically two kinds of musicians: those who obsess over their gear, and those who can't remember the model numbers of their instruments to save their lives. While the former are constantly scouting out new gear and hotly debating their preferences with fellow gearheads, the latter are asking, "Is this thing on?" In my years as a music journalist, I've spent quite a bit of time trying to ferret out the details of what equipment performers are using and why, and my questions are greeted as often with a slightly embarrassed shrug as by a lengthy dissertation on the merits of one gizmo over another.

In my early twenties I went out with a guy who had 13 different guitars, and he used to sit and explain to me the differences among them and what work he had done on which one on that particular day and how he had done this and that to the humbucker and switched a pickup here and there. . . . Once I literally fell asleep while he was talking to me. I thought it was funny when I woke up, but he was not amused.

—Suzanne Vega

Just as encyclopedic knowledge of music theory doesn't in itself lead to good songwriting, there is no correlation between being a gear expert and being a great player. It's the ideas, not the tools, that count. But the fact is, even if you don't understand or think much about gear, you still need to use it to make and share music. In performance, your equipment directly affects how you feel and what people hear.

It's important to have a great sound. We're picky, picky—I mean I can hear a string imbalance in the middle of a crowded bar. It's important to me. And it's not a reflection of being a good player, 'cause I'm not even a good player. The guitar has to be an extension of you in order to perform with it, so it's got to sound great. It can sound great in a crappy bar or a big room. It's not about having the most expensive equipment; it's just that your guitar has to feel like you.

—Amy Ray

When it comes to equipment, there are endless permutations in taste, sophistication, and budget. Obviously the gear considerations are different if you have a crew setting up your Wall of Sound in arenas across the land (hi, Mick!). But for singer-songwriters schlepping themselves and their gear from gig to gig, there are some rules of thumb.

Suzanne Vega

❖ *Keep it simple.* That is, keep your rig as simple as it can be while still delivering what you need it to deliver. Notice that I said *need* and not *want.* With music gear as with any consumer product, it's tricky to distinguish between what is essential and what is just shiny and new and has cool flashing lights, but that's what you have to do. The more you can strip down your rig, the less you have to carry, the quicker the setup, and the lower the odds that something will go wrong. And that all translates into more time for you to concentrate on the music.

Anytime you are thinking about upgrading your equipment, you need to consider the trade-off between sonic improvement and added complexity. If that new black box sounds better than your old black box but requires a lot more tweaking during every sound check, does the result justify the time and effort? Will the audience notice the difference? Will you?

Hand in hand with simplicity is reliability. There's nothing worse than dealing with a piece of equipment that is rattling, buzzing, or failing to emit any sound at a time when you should be mentally preparing for the show you're about to play. So invest a little more for gear that's rugged and reliable, just for the peace of mind. But more expensive isn't necessarily better. Stay away from stuff that sounds great but is finicky and fragile—there are a lot of amazing instruments, microphones, and other musical tools that are used widely in the studio but never onstage (and there's a very good reason why the cheap and nearly indestructible Shure SM57 and SM58 mics are found nearly everywhere music is amplified). It's just a matter of time before a piece of performing gear is dinged, dropped, or spilled on.

❖ *Leave your precious stuff at home.* No matter what instrument or equipment you're toting along to a performance, you have to be prepared for the possibility that it will get lost, stolen, damaged, or ruined. Sorry. The sad truth is that there are thieves, baggage handlers, and even careless friends out in the world who don't have the kinds of personal attachments to your gear that you do. So look at everything you are planning to bring with you and ask yourself the heart-wrenching question, "Can I afford to lose this, psychologically and financially?" If the answer is no, leave it at home. That may mean performing with your not-quite-favorite instrument and pretty good mic, but you will feel less stressed when you travel and more relaxed at the gig. As with all gear matters, you are making a compromise between what inspires you to play your best and what is most suited to the life of hard knocks. If you feel you've got to perform with an instrument of great cash or personal value, go for it—but make that decision with your eyes open.

If your instrument and expensive gear are properly insured, that may change the equation of what you feel comfortable bringing with you. Your homeowner's or renter's insurance might cover your instrument for damage or loss (double-check the details), but probably *not* if you are using it professionally. So a working musician needs special insurance coverage, which you may be able to obtain through membership in a musician's union or performance rights society like ASCAP and BMI.

❖ *Accessorize.* Even the simplest instrument setup requires an assortment of additional gizmos and spare parts. So assemble a compact traveling kit of all the things you might need and, whenever possible, extras: the list might include guitar accessories (strings, string winder, string cutter, picks, capo, nail file), electronic tuner, microphone (and perhaps a windscreen for a vocal mic), direct box, cables, batteries (for preamps, microphones, tuners, etc.), and maybe a few small repair items for your instrument if you are the tinkering sort. Get in the habit of bringing this kit along even if you're just going to the local coffeehouse, and then keeping it within easy reach while you play. It's better to be a little overprepared than to be frantically searching for a new nine-volt battery right before a gig.

❖ *Reduce the variables.* When you line up a show, check what gear will be available at the venue—and prepare for the possibility that it won't actually be there, or that it will be decrepit or dysfunctional. Consider bringing along one or two key items, such as a vocal microphone or a direct box, even if the venue supplies them. That'll make your setup and sound more consistent and—I'm sounding like a broken record here—allow you to focus more on the music and interacting with the audience.

❖ *Maintain your instrument.* Like cars and teeth, musical instruments need regular maintenance to function at their best. They aren't static objects but are constantly changed by the forces of time, string tension, playing, travel, weather, and the seasons. An annual setup on a guitar (or any fretted instrument), for instance, will make it easier and smoother to play, fix any buzzes and rattles, improve the tone and intonation, decrease string breakage, and generally catch small problems before they develop into big problems. That's a minor investment well worth making.

❖ *Listen to your plugged-in tone.* No matter how lovely your instrument sounds when you play it at home, what the audience hears is whatever comes out of the speakers—and for acoustic instruments, that sound is largely determined by your amplification rig. Far too many singer-songwriters wind up with a rubber-band-y tone from their acoustic guitar pickups. You might get away with that in a band, where only a small part of your instrument's tone is cutting through the mix, but in a solo show, it's critical to have a full, pleasing sound.

Amplification systems for acoustic instruments have evolved to the point that you can get a good sound without blowing your bank account, carrying a ton of gear, or having a four-hour sound check—and a cheap instrument with the right pickup system can sound as good or better than a boutique beauty. Also, don't overlook the old-fashioned external microphone: when skillfully used in low-volume settings (especially without drums), an inexpensive mic can deliver an excellent approximation of what the instrument sounds like unplugged.

❖ *Ask other musicians.* By far the best source of information and advice about gear is other musicians who have been there, tried that. You won't have to pry—performers love talking about this stuff and spend many hours backstage trading tips and war stories. Gear preferences are subjective, of course, but at least you are listening to the voices of experience rather than the breathless hyperbole of some company's marketing department.

Other sources of gear advice include musicians' publications, which bring journalistic balance to how-to articles and reviews (and, for better or worse, a more diplomatic tone than what you'll hear in the green room), and Web forums, where strangers sitting at keyboards around the world will tell you exactly what you should buy. Since you know nothing about the real lives or hidden agendas of people posting on the Web, give more weight to widely recurring recommendations than to any individual's foaming-at-the-mouth opinions.

❖ *Find a gear guru.* If you just don't have that gear-obsession gene in you, cultivate a relationship with someone who does. This might be a repairer at the local music store or a fellow player—anyone who understands *your* needs, style, taste, and budget and can steer you toward the equipment that's the best match.

Music stores these days are packed with good products in all price ranges. In the last decade especially, manufacturers have found ways to bring all sorts of high-end gear (e.g., guitars, microphones, digital recording gear) into the reach of musicians on tight budgets. So the challenge isn't so much finding the good stuff as sorting through many, many options, and that's where reliable advice—from other musicians, a shop, a magazine, or wherever—is so valuable.

BOOKING BASICS

You love the writing. You're fascinated by the process of trying to capture your songs on record. You get a big buzz out of performing, and the good nights more than make up for the bad ones. But the booking? You will be hard pressed to find anyone who likes this part of being a working musician—booking is tough, frustrating work, with a lot of slings and arrows to endure for every success.

Booking also happens to be a necessary step if you are ever going to take the stage with your name by the door. And when you're starting out, you really don't have any choice but to buckle down and do it yourself. You may not have any idea what you're doing at first, but you fill all the other job requirements: You know your music better than anyone, and you are its most passionate advocate. You've got the love and the long-term perspective that justifies all the effort for slim financial rewards. You've got every motivation to succeed in the booking business, including perhaps the fervent desire to get to where you don't have to do it anymore—where you've built enough of an audience and buzz that it's financially worthwhile for an agent to represent you.

Booking yourself also gives you a lot of control, contacts, and knowledge, said Rani Arbo, who booked her bands Salamander Crossing and Daisy Mayhem for years.

A lot of the coffeehouses book very much on personal taste and not on hype, because everyone is in it for the love of music and the committees are very invested in having their own personal say in who comes. It's not like a performing arts center where they kind of have to book on hype or on reputation because they are going for a bigger audience, and they don't have the time, they don't have the volunteers, and they don't have the same sort of investment to go through mountains and mountains of stuff in press kits.

So I think the smaller circuit is totally bookable by an individual. It is a lot of work, but on the other hand, it means that when you show up you've actually had conversations with the promoters, you've established a relationship, and if you know the right questions to ask and how to put the contract together, you have an incredible amount of information as to what is going to happen when you get there. For me, dealing with four people and travel and everything, that was actually a source of some comfort.

—Rani Arbo

At the grassroots and local levels, booking is a relatively straightforward (though not easy) process, and it isn't necessarily a disadvantage to be booking yourself—some venues actually prefer dealing directly with artists. The advice I've gleaned from performers, agents, and club bookers can be boiled down to a few simple precepts. See Resources for suggestions on where to find more detailed and specialized information.

❖ *Polish your promo.* A good promotional package tells venue bookers, clearly and concisely, who you are and what your music is like. It relays the message three ways: by what they see, what they hear, and what they read.

The visual presentation has to be crisp and attractive. Sure, we all want to be judged by what we sound like, not what we look like, but a good photo is very important: it should be professionally shot ("not a snapshot of you in your backyard holding a guitar," advised booking agent Nancy Fly) and duplicated as a full-size glossy by one of the many promo photo services. Make sure *you* are the focal point and not the background, so your mug will still be seen if the photo is reproduced at thumbnail size in a calendar or publication. The CD cover art should reflect the identity you're trying to get across, as should the design of the bio/promo page. It's nice if the designs of all these elements tie in together so the whole thing looks and feels like a cohesive package.

If you've released a full CD, that works fine for the audio portion of your promo pack, as long as it's representative of what you do in your live show and the first couple of songs make your musical point (I know it's unfair, but judgments are often made on the basis of brief samplings of one or two tracks). If you've got a strong CD but it's quite different from what you do onstage—if, for instance, it's a band CD but you perform solo—you should supplement it with some songs in the vein of your show. There's nothing like a few live tracks, with wildly enthusiastic applause, to get across the idea that you are not a novice at this gigging business. For promotional purposes, you could make a sampler of studio and live performances. If you've got nothing recorded, well, you need to make a demo of at least three or four tracks— fortunately, it's easy and cheap to make a bare-bones demo these days. Once again, no matter what kind of listening material you include, put your best songs first, because even track 4 might never be spun.

The reading portion of a promo package normally includes a bio, copies of selected reviews and articles, and often a page of quotes compiled from wherever you can get them—press, deejays, people at venues where you've played, other artists. If you're starting out, you may have to do a lot of soliciting to get any usable quotes. Obviously a well-known source gives the quote more impact, but a few words from even an obscure Web site or 'zine adds authority and shows you've been out in the world playing.

Work hard on the bio and other material you write yourself: this is your chance to describe and spin your music in the way that you want to, and often your exact words are reproduced in newspapers or venue calendars. As with all good writing, be specific—evoke sounds and styles that people know. Don't just throw up your hands and say the music is unclassifiable, even if you think that is the case. Classify it in some way yourself, or someone else will (and the result will probably make you wince).

❖ *Do your homework on venues.* As mentioned above, the Web is invaluable for finding places to play. Look up itineraries of artists at your level or slightly above and compile a list of possible venues—and be realistic about where you would fit in stylistically and how big a draw you actually have. Take note of ticket prices too. It's much better to do well at a small venue than to aim too high and wind up with a painfully slow night at a bigger place than you are ready for. Get venue recommendations from other musicians. When you book a gig somewhere away from your home turf, ask the people at that venue to recommend places that you might play on the way in or out. When you call those other venues, be sure to mention where you're already booked—that automatically gives you legitimacy.

Be creative about venues, too, and keep your eyes open for all the sorts of alternatives we discussed earlier in this chapter—house concerts, opening slots, bookstores, and so on. You may need to do some lower profile appearances at first in order to be seriously considered for a full headline slot. No matter how much they like your CD, venue bookers may want to see you play before they schedule you for your own night.

❖ *Call first.* Don't bother mailing anything without first making contact by phone or e-mail and getting the green light. It's a waste of time, postage, and plastic. Everyone in this business is besieged by promo material, and the majority of it winds up in the circular file.

When you first contact a venue, briefly introduce yourself and ask simply if they are accepting material and who you should send it to. If you can't connect with the actual booking person, someone else at the venue can probably give you this information and tell you when/where you might follow up. (If you send an e-mail but it goes unanswered, as often happens, try the phone during business hours.) Get the name of the person you speak to, and when you send your package, attach a note saying that you spoke to so-and-so, who suggested you send the material along. Referencing that contact and the go-ahead to send your promo raises the odds of your package getting a look and a listen.

❖ *Follow up.* Until you get to be famous, you have to do more than call, send your package, and wait for the phone to ring with offers for high-paying and glamorous gigs. You have to call again a couple weeks later. And call again. And call again. And call again. And call again . . . You may feel like they're being rude or you're being a pest, but you are just doing what you have to do, because there are many other musicians and agents trying to get the attention of the same individual. No response doesn't mean that your promo has been carefully checked out and deemed inappropriate for the venue; it means that your package is still sitting in a pile unopened, or (best-case scenario) that your promo *did* get checked out and placed into a pile of possibilities, where it will forever remain unless you follow up. Gigs go to those who persist.

When you're going through this process, you have to steel yourself against being ignored and rejected over and over again, and keep at it. It's really hard and it really sucks, but try not to take it personally; it's more a reflection of the crowded world around you than it is a judgment of your music. If you're feeling very discouraged, talk to another musician struggling with the same thing—it'll raise your spirits. (You also might check out a little book called *Rotten Reviews and Rejections,* which compiles scathing commentaries on books subsequently deemed to be classics.)

> *You should not expect to be treated with basic courtesy by venue bookers. They will usually not return phone calls or e-mails or listen to and evaluate your music on its merits. But if you persist, you will find gigs, however modest, and if you do well at those gigs, you'll find your audience. You may find bigger and less jaded audiences off the beaten path. Build your audience one at a time, and those real human connections will sustain you.*
>
> —Andrew Calhoun

❖ *Band together.* As you try to make headway in the world of booking, it's very easy to fall prey to feelings of intense competition and jealousy toward your fellow musicians. It's true that there are many, many of you out there trying to do basically the same thing, but musicians have so much to gain by cooperating with each other. Other singer-songwriters are people with whom you can share bills, contacts, tips, and travel expenses; they understand your crazy quest and are your best support group and source of comic relief.

You can band together professionally to do things that would be very difficult or impossible to do on your own. Many singer-songwriters have successfully co-headlined shows (your audience plus her audience equals enough bodies to fill a bigger room), done group tours (organized by label, region, stylistic affinity, or just friendship), put together compilation CDs, and collectively put on showcases at industry events that are prohibitively expensive to do alone. Sometimes they wind up creating a formal organization. The Austin Conspiracy, for example, is a group of performing songwriters (with membership by invitation only) that sponsors showcases at Folk Alliance and South by Southwest, shares gigging tips and information at monthly meetings and via an e-mail list, organizes group shows, and runs a Web site. Indiegrrl is a networking organization for women performers that at this writing boasts 1,800 members (mainly singer-songwriters). Affiliations and collectives of all sorts have become common in the indie music world, and for good reason: there's power in numbers.

❖ *Get organized.* The more gigs you do, the more you need to develop a system for organizing all the information associated with booking them: contact information for the various people at the venue (booker, manager, sound guy), directions, sound check and performance time, equipment needs, capacity, the financial deal, ticket price, anything else supplied (food and drink, groupies, green M&Ms), places to stay, local press and radio contacts for publicity . . . It's a good idea to keep a checklist of these items in an electronic file so you can e-mail it or fill it out as you're talking on the phone. That way, you and the venue booker are clear on the details, and you know what to ask for and what to expect when you show up. (A side benefit is that you've probably impressed the venue with your professionalism.) A lot of these details might be formalized in a contract, too; the venue may have a standard contract, or you can create a performer-friendly contract by adapting one from another musician/agent or using a published sample (see Resources).

Paper files or a notebook will work fine for a small amount of booking information, but the more you perform the more time you'll save by going electronic. Eventually, you may want to build the kind of database that an agent would use or buy a program specifically designed for that purpose.

❖ *Build on your success.* If you want to gain some momentum as a performer and step up to the next level, keep in mind that a scattershot approach to gigging will take you only so far. The same principle discussed above for opening slots—that you should always have a follow-up plan—applies to all the gigs you do. Rather than randomly chase down whatever gig possibilities pop up, wherever they may be, you can follow a general game plan in which one show builds on the last and the one before. Here's one such scenario, described by Brandon Kessler of the indie label Messenger Records.

> *When you're starting out, try to build a regional following around your hometown. Start by booking shows at home, then build outward in concentric circles. It's important to revisit the cities where you have played, as you want to keep the momentum going. Make sure to promote your shows. Call the promoter at the club and ask for a local media list for press and radio. Send them CDs and a bio with the tour date listed, and follow up with them.*
>
> *If you work hard to promote the shows (i.e., hand out flyers, contact the press and radio, and get posters and flyers displayed around town and at the local record stores), the promoters will notice. They will be encouraged to give you better shows on better nights of the week with bands that draw more people. If you work diligently, and people like your music and are willing to pay to see you, you can build a regional following. Then you can network with artists in other regions and offer to trade shows with them (they can open for you and vice versa). And then, of course, you want to revisit the cities where you've played.*
>
> *I can't stress enough the importance of selling CDs at the show, keeping a mailing list at the show, and letting people know your Web address by handing out flyers. The mailing list is absolutely crucial, as your following is everything.*
>
> —Brandon Kessler

The real world is always unpredictable, for good and bad, and performers need to be ready to jump on unexpected opportunities as well as recover from unexpected calamities. But a thought-out plan helps focus your efforts on gigs that pave the way for better gigs down the road.

AGENTS AND HELPERS

Let's say you've gotten yourself off the ground as a performer. You've played a widening circle of clubs and have a CD out, some press clips, and a growing mailing list, and now the opportunity presents itself to get some help with the booking. Before you kick up your heels and happily turn over booking responsibilities, it's important to understand the workings of this relationship from both sides.

Perhaps there is someone else who loves your music nearly as much as you do, a friend or fan or patron saint who volunteers to pitch in. Should you take up the offer of this kind soul, who's got great intentions but knows nothing about the music business? Here are a couple of perspectives on that question, first from singer-songwriter Andrew Calhoun, who founded the artists' cooperative label Waterbug Records, then from booking agent Jim Fleming, who has represented artists from the coffeehouse level on up through a star attraction like Ani DiFranco.

What I saw with Waterbug was that every single time that artists got help with booking (with the exception of major players like Fleming/Tamulevich), they ended up with big holes in their schedules because the agent dropped the ball. There isn't enough money at this level to attract and motivate quality professionals. You need to bite the bullet and do all your own booking and promotion, until such time as there is such demand for you that you haven't got time to do it. Which may never happen. It's a lousy office/sales job just like any other, but it will allow you to practice your art. When people offer help, let them gather contacts, then follow up yourself, because chances are, they won't.

—Andrew Calhoun

If you can find a person who is as passionate about your music as you are, has some business skills, and is smart and willing to learn, that could be somebody very valuable for you to form a relationship with. I believe that as in any relationship, the key thing is to be patient. You stay in touch with each other frequently and acknowledge what the hurdles are and what problems you are having, and acknowledge your shortcomings too.

The thing that I have heard consistently over the years from artists is that it's really hard for them to get on the phone and sell themselves, and that's why they want someone else selling for them. But the fact is, if they've gotten to the point where someone is interested in representing them, they have *sold themselves and know much more about that than the person who's going to take it over. Use that information to teach. In a way I think it's valuable to do it yourself for a long time, because then you are able to tell if that person is doing a good job or not.*

—Jim Fleming

Booking is, as Andrew Calhoun noted, a sales job, and if you're going to be represented by someone who does this for a living, you need to consider the hard numbers. For many performers, there just isn't all that much money involved. Booking agents work on a percentage basis: 15 percent, or maybe 20 for a less-established artist. The artist typically supplies everything that goes into promo mailings—CDs, photos, printed material—while the agent covers postage, phone calls, and the like. With this arrangement, lining up low-paying shows can be a case of what booking agent Nancy Fly called "rabbit starvation."

Rabbit starvation is where it takes more energy to hunt, kill, dress, and cook the rabbit than you gain in nutrition when you eat it. So a lot of gigs that we book for a brand-new artist, if the artist is making $100 or $150, we're losing money, because it costs more than our 15 percent to book the date. But that's still something *that we are willing to do if we feel that the artist is going to devel-op and will be able to make $2,000 to $2,500 pretty soon, and then we'll be in the black again. So that's why I say when you are a developing artist, you have to get somebody who's absolutely in love with what you do, or you've got to do it yourself.*

—Nancy Fly

Of course, the agent isn't the only one affected by rabbit star-vation. If you are making $100 a show, does it really makes sense to hand $15 or $20 over to an agent? More to the point, is this agent accomplishing something that you couldn't do yourself? Just as agents are sometimes willing to work for a mea-ger fee in the short term because they see potential in the longer term, the rabbit-starvation scenario makes sense for you only if you believe the agent will eventually land better-paying, higher-visibility gigs than you could line up yourself. It's worth keep-ing in mind that an agent with low overhead (working solo or part time from a home office) can afford to invest more time and effort in developing your career than can someone at a larg-er agency, with rent and payroll and all the other office expenses to meet each month.

This is a business relationship between you and an agent, and you need to treat it as such. But, as I've said, when you are estab-lishing yourself as a performer, you want to work with someone who sees more than dollar signs in the future. An agent or publi-cist with a passion for your music will do a much better job sell-ing you, and will be much more patient and persistent at the early stages. The higher you rise on the music business ladder, the less important this passion becomes—at some point, the money is enough to justify the agent's effort. With big stars, booking becomes a matter of negotiating rather than selling; the music has already proved itself and found its audience.

If a professional agent sees enough potential in your career to justify working for a while at the rabbit-starvation level, he or she understandably wants some kind of guarantee that you won't skip off to another agent as soon as you're established. That's why an agent agreement might include a term: say, three years, after which the agreement might be renewed or terminated. Before signing an agreement like this, be sure you understand exactly what is expected of you and what is expected of the agent. And in *any* long-term agreement, advised lawyer Wayne Rooks (whose firm has represented such independent spirits as Ani DiFranco, Moby, and Pete Seeger), build in as many "out clauses" as possible, so you don't get stuck if specific benchmarks are not met.

A good agent brings contacts and experience in the booking business beyond what you have, and opens doors that you as an independent artist could bang on all day without having anybody answer. But don't expect an agent to—poof!—perform miracles. Just as gigging is only one facet of being a singer-songwriter, the booking agent is one cog in a bigger wheel.

It doesn't really make sense to get a booking agent until you are trying to promote a CD nationally. And a booking agent is part of a whole team: you need to have national publicity, national distribution, and a national booking agent all at the same time. A booking agent is not going to do much with you if your record's not getting any airplay and if you don't have anybody calling the radio station and setting up on-air interviews for you and things like that, because nobody will come to your gig. You might be able to get a gig once, but nobody will ever ask you back.

—Nancy Fly

And none of these things—the gigs, the publicity, the distribution—happens without the great songs and the gift for connecting with an audience. Take care of the business, but don't let it sidetrack you from what's truly essential: getting better and better at your art. Even (or especially) in this marketing-saturated age, there is no more powerful advertising than word of mouth, carried by those who leave a show with that special glow from a night of great music.

> *What's the work of a poet? To write poetry. What's the work of an artist? To paint. What's the work of a singer? To sing.*
>
> *Fasten totally on the work. Give yourself completely to the work, till you can do it as well as it can be done, and then people come looking for you. But forget the rest of it. That will happen if you're completely fixed on the work. It's a superstition, I know; I believe it.*
>
> —Utah Phillips

IN THE STUDIO

When I first got the songwriting bug and the attendant desire to capture my creations on tape (dateline 1977), the four-track cassette recorder seemed like a godsend. It was such a leap beyond the boombox with the tinny built-in mic, allowing fledgling songwriters such as my brother and I to try out some of the rhythm and harmony ideas that were beyond the capability of two voices and four hands. With a borrowed bass and drum machine (featuring ultracheesy handclaps that were completely irresistible), it was possible to simulate on a crude and sometimes comical level the backup band we fantasized about having.

But as cool as all this was, the hissy sounds of the multitrack cassette could not be confused with the glossy productions coming from my favorite LPs. That was the realm of the professionals—of pop stars and masterful studio cats laying down tracks with mixing consoles as big as my bedroom. With few exceptions, home recording was for personal expression; the major labels held the keys to the world of commercial recording, opening the studio doors only to those with holy-grail record deals and big budgets.

The reality for musicians today is startlingly different. Plenty of high-profile pop music still comes from those slick players, fancy studios, and major labels, but professional-quality recordings can come from anywhere else too. With the arrival of the DAT machine in the '80s, high-quality live digital recording became possible in any living room or at any gig; with the ADAT, multi-track digital recording came within the reach of home studio mavens with a bit more money and ambition. Those twin inventions let the genie out of the bottle, and nowadays a little box or computer is practically all you need to make a simple recording worthy of anyone's CD player. You can record on your own time, at your own pace, and for a whole array of purposes beyond making a full-length CD: to work on new songs, to experiment with arrangements, to make a demo, to collaborate, or simply to share songs with friends and family.

Chris Smither

These changes in recording technology have fed right into the growth of independent and artist-owned labels from a fringe phenomenon to a significant and far-reaching channel for new music. A big part of that story, too, is the development of the Internet and its powerful tools for interacting and doing business directly with music fans. So along with the major labels and their marketing power, there are many other tiers in the record business today, from large independents with multiple subsidiary labels on down through individual artists selling self-financed, self-produced, self-released CDs off the stage and from self-designed Web sites. In other words, this is a world of many options and opportunities beyond waiting for a megacorporation to come along and turn your songs into gold records and Grammys. A new kind of power—and responsibility—is in your hands.

When I first started, you hoped and prayed and worked and hopefully you'd get a record deal. There was no such thing as making your own record or doing any of the things that you can do now to start a career and work it on your own. There's been a radical change. The technology and access to dissemination, either through the Internet or any other ways, have made it so much more of a do-it-yourself thing, with people building viable careers when on the surface no one has ever heard of them. To me it's remarkable.

—Chris Smither

You can actually sell or give or share your music with the whole world. You don't have to have the middleman. Availability has always been the trick gate that record companies have stood in front of. For most musicians, it's like, "You can only get through this gate through me." So then it means, "You have to jump through this hoop first, and then I'll let you go in." You don't really have to go through that anymore. You can make your own Web site and get your music out there. And a lot of people are doing it, and much to their surprise, doing it well. It comes down to this: if the music is good and it has something to say and it has something to offer a listener, then that listener has the wonderful ability to make that choice. He wants it, he gets it.

I can tell you for a fact that in the 1960s, for every hit song or every hit group that made an album, I probably would much rather have the demo they gave the company than the album the company made. It's still the same. Make your own music. Get the atmosphere around that song that you want. And the people will hear it and will feel it.

—Richie Havens

Even as the tools and the business of recording have changed in fundamental ways, the creative challenge remains the same. How do you take these living, breathing songs of yours and convey their essence in a fixed medium? Should you dress them up with other instruments or present them as you wrote them? Where is the magic balance between sounding polished and professional and nitpicking all the life out of your tracks? How do you communicate with fellow human beings when you're sitting alone with headphones on staring at a microphone grille? And how do you make the technology serve the music rather than the other way around?

More than ever, the artist is the one answering these questions, rather than a producer or manager or A&R department. There is no one-size-fits-all scenario for recording—each artist and each project is unique. But there are key issues, some philosophical and others purely practical, that every recording musician needs to address. Some of the most important decisions are made long before you press the record button, so let's start back in the planning stages.

GETTING READY TO RECORD

There is something seductive about having your own CD. I'll never forget the moment I finished burning the first copy of a home-recorded collection of my songs and popped it into the CD player. Those track numbers and the orange numbers ticking off the seconds gave me an instant feeling that after more than 20 years of playing and writing songs, I was finally a *real musician.*

Friends and fans, too, reinforce the feeling that having a tangible, saleable product of your own is the sign of being serious about your art. They will urge you to make your first CD and your next and your next, and you want to satisfy them—and yourself. So the desire and the motivation to record are often very powerful, and the technology that makes it happen is within reach.

Richie Havens

In the flush of excitement about amazing gear and shiny discs, however, one essential question is often glossed over: not "What should I record?" or "How should I record?" but "Why am I recording?" As noted above, there are many potential purposes for a recording project. Know before you start why you are doing it, and keep that intention in your sights. The process of capturing sounds, turning knobs and sliding sliders, and hearing a song take shape is so absorbing that it is easy to forget why you're doing it—and you emerge weeks or months later, bleary-eyed and broke, with something that doesn't really do what you set out to do, and with important projects (like new songs) left unfinished.

The first thing to realize is that the world already contains a staggering amount of recorded music, much of it piling up on closet shelves or sitting in dusty boxes. I personally have been on the receiving end of review copies of CDs for years—more music than I could ever hope to check out fully while still eating, sleeping, and making a living. Music critics like to pretend that they hear everything and know exactly which records and artists are the best, but if they were honest they would admit that great music escapes their attention every day while they rave about other music that they may barely remember by next month. I've heard more than a few people in the music business joke about the need for a law requiring musicians to wait a certain number of years before making a CD, like waiting to buy a handgun. It can be depressing to think about this, but it's a truth that must be acknowledged.

The flip side is that none of the other stuff out there is *your* music, and there's always room for another voice and another creation. At some point, you need to block out everything else and throw yourself into making the music that only you can make. But if you want to make a record for distribution and sale to the general public, be sure that it meets two criteria: you are ready, and the material is ready. Consider these thoughts from two people in the record business: Jim Olsen, head of the singer-songwriter–

oriented indie label Signature Sounds, and Dawn Atkinson, formerly with Windham Hill and Imaginary Road Records and at this writing an independent producer and A&R person working with BMG's RCA Victor group.

Don't rush your art. I really feel like many songwriters are in such a rush and fall in love with the recording process so that before they know it they have four or five records that have sold minimally. The industry doesn't care, and the audience is a little confused because they don't know which record to buy.

I think an artist needs to be out there testing the material live. Just because you have ten songs doesn't mean it's time to make a record. Maybe you press up a bare-bones demo record with just you and guitar so you have something to sell at gigs and give to club owners and such. But hold off on that debut album until you feel like this is a piece of work that really represents the best that you can do. And when you do cut that album, realize that until people hear it, it's a new record. It can be a new record for two or three years. Make sure you work it from every angle so you get as many people to hear it as possible before you create a glut of product that doesn't really have an audience yet.

—Jim Olsen

Don't make a record until all the songs are great. There are certain artists that I can remember working with whose first record was fabulous, the second record was pretty good, the third record was worse, and they start making too many too often. They become better at their craft of writing songs but not necessarily better at the quality of the songs. They've had a whole lifetime to collect material for their first record, and then they have a year and a half, or however long it is, to do the next one. Maybe they have some rejects from the first album, but they all of a sudden have a time frame that they have to write in. That's a big problem, because what if you don't come up with great songs in that time frame?

What do you do—postpone your album release, or just put some-
thing out because you want to keep the momentum of your career
going? A record company would say, put something out. I think
that's wrong. I think you are better off working on it longer.
    I think that's the hardest thing—keeping up the great songs.
And then also, don't be afraid to sing someone else's great song.

                      —Dawn Atkinson

As Jim Olsen suggested, it is possible to meet the demand for a
recording to sell at gigs and use as a promotional demo while still
waiting for the right moment to unveil your "official" debut. In
fact, making a recording or two without the pressure of making
the recording is a very good idea. Especially if you are used to live
performance, the studio might seem like an alien environment for
making music. You're sitting in front of highly sensitive microphones, your ears encased in thick headphones, conscious of the
need to deliver something special while trying not to worry about
the time (and money) ticking away. Without an audience, you
have to generate your own energy and communicate with people
you can't see, who may not hear what you are playing until years
later. Here's how two accomplished performers described the conceptual leap that you have to make to get your best music on
record.

It's a very different mental process. You have to really concentrate
on where you're sending your energy. It's not as obvious, so it takes
more focus. You have to imagine that you're sending your music
not at the microphone, but into the microphone and into the wire
and into the machinery and into the tape and into the speakers
and into the person and into the heart.

                      —David Wilcox

I remember back when I used to do the Prairie Home *show, I was*
always fascinated with the fact that Garrison [Keillor] seemed to

have such a sense of the radio audience, and I never really did. I was just playing to those people there in the World Theater or wherever we were, and he had this remarkable sense of people out there in their yards or in their living room or on a boat, listening to the show. I might have learned something from him about that, about being able to imagine when you're making a record that you are playing for people.

—Greg Brown

Studio playing also requires very close attention to sonic detail. In this laboratory-like environment, mistakes that nobody would notice during a live show can be distracting and bothersome. Some of your best tricks onstage might not hold up under the scrutiny of a recorded take that will be heard again and again and again; by the same token, there are nuances you can exploit in the studio that would be completely lost in performance. When you're recording, you have to play and sing more cleanly than usual, yet you need to be loose enough that your take has soul and guts. It takes time to adjust to all this, explained the veteran session player, producer, performer, and recording artist Jerry Douglas.

The studio is a different place to play music than the stage. You're not getting feedback from the audience. Every note you play is under a microscope, but the cool thing about it is, you get more chances if you need them. It goes both ways: I know a lot of recording musicians who say, "Oh, I can't play in a band in a live situation—I am just not good at it." And with a lot of road musicians, you get them in the studio and you start hearing things that you didn't hear live—maybe some rough edges, a lot of noise, things that you just can't do in the studio.

It depends on what kind of music you are playing, I guess, but if you are trying to be smooth and you're trying to fit into a track, you want to really listen to other people and try to play as cleanly as possible. Try to put the best thing on tape that you can with a low noise ratio. And that's really hard for a lot of people who come in and don't know how to sit in front of a microphone, who've never played in a band situation sitting down or with headphones on. If you want a consistent sound on your instrument or on your vocal, you can't be jumping around like you've got an SM58 in your hand onstage.

—Jerry Douglas

You don't want to be learning these lessons while renting studio time. It's very discouraging, not to mention expensive, to deliver a spot-on performance and then discover that it was ruined by your squeaking chair or explosive *p*-pop in your vocal mic. So set yourself up at home to make practice tapes: work on your microphone technique, sing while wearing headphones (if it feels really strange, try using the headphones on only one ear), and if you're planning

Jerry Douglas

to overdub parts, practice with some basic multitrack gear. Listen critically to the results, and correct any problems you find.

Practice tapes also present the opportunity to assess the state of the material, make some final edits, and experiment with arrangements. How well do the songs translate? What other sounds might be needed to bring them alive? Are any lyrics not quite there yet? Is the song structure tight, or are there places where you need to add or subtract?

> In songwriting workshops I tell people, [imagine] if a painter said, "Well, now I'm going to go paint my masterpiece without any sketches and without any little plans." It took me a long time to figure out that if you get the recording equipment—just a little simple setup—and tape the stuff and listen back to it, or goof around with arrangements before you go into the studio, it's really helpful.
> —Patty Larkin

While these tapes (or demos or whatever you prefer to call them) can help you work through questions and streamline the process that will follow, don't fuss too much over them, overdubbing lots of parts and trying to perfect every last note. Think of a demo as a sketchpad rather than your final canvas, a place to clarify and capture your ideas. A sketch that is too carefully rendered begins to compete with the artwork it's supposed to support.

> Demos are dangerous, because you create a good demo, and then you're trying to re-create it when you get into the studio or when you get onstage, and that's difficult. I don't like doing that. You can't finish a song on a demo. You should just throw down the idea and "That's it, we'll get to it later," because those lame drum beats can really take all the fun out of a good song.
> —Alana Davis

As you plot out a full-length recording project, make sure you take a step back to consider how well the material as a whole hangs together. It's tempting to try to pack everything that you can do onto a record—particularly your first—but you might wind up with what producer Malcolm Burn called the "Kellogg's variety pack" ("Here's our fast song and here's our slow song and here's our country song and here's our reggae song"). There's something so powerful about a record with a point of view. It's like a house with a distinctive look and style when viewed from the street; inside, each song is a room that has its own purpose and decor but relates back to the overall architecture. Your opening song invites people in the front door, then track by track, you lead them on a walking tour of the interior. Listeners can really lose themselves in a record like that.

Considering your recording project in this light also forces you to think about who those listeners are—or who you hope they will be. Can you picture a particular person or group of people grooving to the CD you're going to make? Are you creating a keepsake for fans of your solo show, building a band sound for rock-oriented listeners, trying to cultivate a new audience? Imagining your listeners will help inspire soulful performances and guide you through what can be a byzantine process.

Perhaps the ultimate example of the targeted audience approach is the songwriting demo, made expressly for pitching a song to another artist to record. In music business centers like Nashville and L.A., an entire industry is built up around making demos for professional and wannabe songwriters. While songwriting demos these days typically feature full-band instrumentation to give producers a taste of what the final record might sound like, they are an entirely different animal from records made for commercial release. The goal is not to highlight the unique personality of the songwriter, but to present a recording artist with a perfect vessel into which to pour his or her own personality—it's like pitching a screenplay to a movie star with a tailor-made (and sexy and heroic and touching and otherwise incredibly flattering) starring role. This gives a certain slant not only to how a song is recorded but

to which song is selected in the first place, pointed out Kyle Staggs
of Bug Music, which pitches songs by a long list of singer-songwriters for covers by other artists as well as for use in film, TV, and
other media.

> *Singer-songwriters generally write very personal songs. It's a
> cathartic thing for them—they're writing about their lives, about
> their friend's lives. So sometimes these songs are not really cover-
> able by someone else because somebody else hasn't had the same
> life experiences. Or the song is not usable in a film because even
> though the sentiment is perfect, the words don't fit the scene that's
> going on. Music supervisors are very conscious of the words in a
> song.*
>
> *That having been said, I think that most singer-songwriters have
> a song here or a song there that doesn't really fit in those parame-
> ters. They write a song that's a little less personal or that's so per-
> sonal but applicable to a whole wide range of people, or it has a
> big instrumental section in the middle or something like that; and
> all of a sudden a music supervisor is interested in it or someone
> could cover that song.*
>
> —Kyle Staggs

When it comes to making a demo of a song that fits these
requirements, marketing considerations influence the sound and
feel of the track. The demo might feature a singer hired for a general (but not *too* close) similarity to whoever the song is going to
be pitched to. Sometimes there are multiple demos—one with a
male singer and one with a female singer, or perhaps one with a
full band and one with piano and vocal, each made to appeal to
particular producers or artists. Songwriters like Beth Nielsen
Chapman who double as singer-songwriters (and there are very
few who successfully straddle these two worlds) are highly conscious of the difference between recording a song for themselves
and for someone else.

When I go to make a demo of a song, I'm not going to necessarily make my record of it. I'm going to put it in a mold that is less defined by my voice, and I wouldn't put like a tuba on it or a conch shell. . . .

I don't really tell people they should go get a whole [fully produced] demo, because sometimes the song is not good enough. Especially an aspiring writer might still be in development; they go and spend thousands of dollars, and as they say in Nashville, "You can't polish a turd."

—Beth Nielsen Chapman

HOME VS. STUDIO RECORDING

As noted above, one of the biggest benefits of the digital revolution is that high-quality recordings can be made just about anywhere. Browsing my own shelves, I find CDs recorded in studios of all sizes, on stages of all sizes, in living rooms and kitchens and basements, in churches, in an empty theater, in a cabin in the woods, on a subway bench . . . Many recordings are made in different environments at different points in the process: basic tracks are done at home, then edited, mixed, and mastered in the studio; solo tracks are recorded one place, then overdubbing and the rest happens somewhere else; and many other variations. The point is, you can customize the process however you want—the technology is ready to travel.

What you're looking for is a recording site that makes you feel comfortable and creative, that inspires you to play your best and has the technical capability to capture that moment. For some, recording in the wee hours at home might summon the most powerful tracks; for others, being in a pro studio may give a heightened intensity and excitement to the whole endeavor. So what's the best environment for you and your project? Here are some important trade-offs to consider.

❖ *Your own time vs. borrowed time.* When you book studio time, unless you are in the enviable position of having many hours and dollars at your disposal in which to fiddle and daydream and wait for inspiration to strike, you have to rise to the occasion when the red recording light goes on. You are on a schedule, and you have to be focused and efficient. Even if you woke up on the wrong side of the bed and don't feel much like playing music that day, you have to get yourself in the mood: it's stand and deliver.

On the other hand, presumably the studio came with an engineer, so you are relieved of the burden of running cables and twiddling knobs, and you can concentrate on playing the music. I

Beth Nielsen Chapman

remember home recording sessions with my band when it took so many hours to get set up in the evening (after our respective day jobs) that by the time we were ready to record it was two in the morning, we were exhausted, and the beginning of the *next* work-day was looming. The gear was finally ready to capture good takes, but we were no longer able to deliver them. By contrast, a skilled engineer in a pro studio will quickly dial in the sounds so your energy doesn't wither while you chase down mysterious buzzes and do test take after test take.

Perhaps the biggest advantage of a home studio is that you can record songs whenever you feel like it. And if you try one night and everything sounds really lame, you can just do it again another night—and the knowledge that you *can* redo things will probably loosen you up and encourage you to take more chances whenever you play. Ideally, you have a dedicated space for home recording and can leave the gear set up, or your gear is simple enough that you can set up and lay down a song before the inspiration fades.

When you have your own place, it's like your laboratory. You can experiment with it. No matter how much you rent a studio, very few people will really go in there and spend two days experimenting. When I built this [home studio], we spent a day trying to find the right place in the room to put the bass.... And since most of what I do is the same kind of instruments, now I have places worked out.

—David Grisman

Speaking of time: when you are budgeting time for a recording project, no matter where you are going to record, I suggest that you make your best guess about how long it's going to take, and then double it. That'll give you a reasonable estimate of the time actually needed. Recording sucks you into a twilight zone where hours and days disappear without a trace.

❖ *Buying vs. renting gear.* In a rented studio, other people are responsible for buying the recording gear and learning how to use it. When something breaks, they need to fix it. When something better comes along, they have to decide whether it's worth the investment. That's a huge responsibility to take on, and it can quickly lead to gear obsession and what producer Gurf Morlix (Lucinda Williams, Slaid Cleaves, Robert Earl Keen) called the "money-pit studio syndrome." Leaving gear matters in somebody else's hands allows you, once again, to focus on writing and playing the music, which is more than enough to keep you busy.

But if you always rent or borrow gear for recording, you do not, as the Marxists say, own the means of production. You are not entirely in control of the recording process, and you're not really learning its inner workings. Now, is that a good thing or a bad thing? It depends on your gear personality—are you a gearhead, gear challenged, or somewhere in between? One strategy that makes sense for a lot of musicians is assembling a basic recording rig at home for songwriting demos, practice recordings, and straightforward solo tracks, but heading for the studio for more complicated ensemble work and productions. Another possibility is to supplement a home recording setup with rented or borrowed equipment (better microphones and preamps, other instruments, etc.) when it comes time to do a full-length project. If you work on a platform at home that's also used in studios (like Pro Tools or ADAT), you can tote your disks or tapes from home to studio and back again and get the best of both worlds.

If you do decide to put together a home studio, be prepared for the sinking feeling you will get when the piece of gear you bought last year—when the pro-audio gurus agreed that it was the best deal out there—is suddenly considered to be, well, last year's model. Recording technology changes as fast as computer technology—

which makes sense considering that much of it *is* computer technology. Look for equipment that has proven its value and quality over a period of years, not months, and that can be upgraded rather than tossed out when the time comes. And remember that there's a lot to be said for really knowing a particular piece of gear (and a particular room) inside and out, so you can just plug and play rather than begin the learning curve all over again with something new.

For acoustic recording at home, the best investment you can make is in high-quality microphones and mic preamps. They never become obsolete, and they have a much more significant impact on the recorded sound than does your platform—in the digital realm, ADAT, a hard-disk recorder, a computer, or whatever you use will deliver good sound. The first time I recorded at home with good microphones, I was amazed at how straightforward the whole process became. I just pointed the mics in the general direction of whatever noise I was making, and they sounded sweet—the baseline quality was high enough that further experimentation was purely optional. And with really nice sounds going down the mic cables at the beginning of the signal chain, many of the fancy effects and mixing functions I had at my disposal became unnecessary. As the saying goes: garbage in, garbage out. The corollary is true too: good stuff in, good stuff out.

❖ *Simplicity vs. versatility.* From my perspective, you should record with the simplest setup that allows you to do what you need to do. Endless options can so easily lead to endless futzing: filling all those extra tracks just because they're there, trying this and that and the other effect even though the first one sounded pretty damn good, and so on. It's fun and fruitful to experiment with new ideas, but too much of that can sidetrack you from serving the song. Technical limitations can be good for creativity, because they force you to rely more on the auditory receptors attached to the sides of your head.

You can make a record on a ghetto blaster if you need to. You can make a record for any amount of money, and it can still be good. You don't have to have state-of-the-art gear. Basically I think you have to have ears. My studio is somewhat limited. It's in a house. I don't have a bunch of great gear. I've got a few nice preamps and a couple of nice microphones. But I feel like the limitations of that really help me keep things simple.

—Gurf Morlix

If your project is focused entirely or primarily on your solo sound, your recording setup can be dead simple and located just about anywhere. If you're using microphones with acoustic instruments or amplifiers, the room has to be quiet enough that your music isn't drowned out by traffic and neighbor noise (and if you're using an amp, you shouldn't drown out the neighbors either!). It's when you start introducing other instruments and people—particularly drums—that a full-fledged studio becomes much easier to work in. Issues of soundproofing and isolation of instruments have already been addressed there, and if you want to do something similar at home you'll have to spend a lot of time propping up mattresses and devising other sound-deadening baffles. The more instruments you're dealing with, the happier you'll be to have the additional tracks, microphones, and other gear available in a studio.

❖ ***Isolation vs. togetherness.*** Engineers generally like having clean separation of sounds, with each instrument on its own track and bleeding onto the other tracks as little as possible. This way, they can easily edit and process each track without interfering with the others. In terms of the recording environment, this means that they will want to build the song track by track or to isolate you and the other musicians with walls, windows, and baffles. If you're accustomed to jamming in a circle in the living room, it can be disorienting to have your bandmates disappear from view and be audible only in your headphones, or to barely glimpse them over walls of mattresses, blankets, and foam. The way you set up to record is always a compromise: sometimes you have to sacrifice a little sonic isolation to create a better ensemble feel, and vice versa.

Any approach to ensemble recording can work. But the point is, in choosing *where* to record you should think about *how* you'll to be able to play in that space—a function of layout and location as well as the capabilities of the equipment.

ENGINEERING AND PRODUCING

The recording environment is more than the room and the gear— it's defined by whoever is working with you. The technology these days encourages musicians to be self-sufficient, taking the tools and the process into their own hands. I once carried this concept to the logical extreme, recording, mixing, and mastering a dozen songs in the living room on a digital multitrack studio; I even designed the artwork on the computer, printed the covers and tray cards and CD labels, and burned a small stack of CDs to package and give to friends and family. It was a thrilling and taxing process—I'm not a technophobe, but my eyes start to glaze over at the very mention of impedance and parameters, and for most parts of this process, I had close to zero knowledge and experience to draw on. So was it possible to do the whole thing myself? Yes, thanks to intelligently designed technology and some very patient friends. Did it come out well? Yes. Would it have come out better with hands-on help from people who actually know how to do this stuff? Absolutely. But if I'd had to rely on and pay others to help me, would I ever have embarked on this project or gotten it done? Hmm . . . Perhaps not.

As the songwriter and performer, you are already wearing a cou- ple of big hats. Is it possible or advisable to also take on the roles of engineer and/or producer? That's an important question, and it begs another: What do those people actually *do* in the studio anyway?

The job of the engineer is more straightforward and consistent from studio to studio and project to project. The engineer is in charge of setting up the gear and dialing in the sounds; it's a technical job but a musical one too, because the shape and impact of the notes you play and sing are at stake. Producers are involved with all this stuff too, but the real nuts and bolts are in the hands of the engineer. If there's no producer, the engineer works directly with the artist in making his or her ideas happen. This can be an appealing arrangement for experienced musicians who know what they want to achieve in the studio and how to communicate their preferences. Over the years I paid several visits to the storied home studio of mandolinist David Grisman in northern California, where he worked with a young engineer who knew the gear and the space inside out. When an impromptu session arose—as it frequently did when Jerry Garcia or another of Grisman's pals stopped by—the engineer needed only a short time to get ready to roll tape, so the musicians were free to just *play*. The recordings that came out of that room clearly reflected the atmosphere of casual creativity.

Compared to the engineer, the producer is a more mysterious figure. Producers are often attributed with tremendous powers: they're credited as the alchemists behind chart-topping albums and blamed for commercial and creative disasters, as if the artists themselves were only tangentially involved. Joni Mitchell once said the producer "laminates you to the popular sounds of your time" and that producing her own records allowed her to remain true to her compositional instincts. Yet producers themselves sometimes describe their role in much humbler terms; in the words of T Bone Burnett, "A lot of what a producer does is make tea."

Broadly speaking, the producer's job is to get the best possible album out of an artist. That involves particular sets of skills and tactics for each artist and each project, but there are some commonalities in what producers do.

❖ *Help select and shape the material.* We've already talked about the editing and filtering of songs you need to do to get ready to record. A producer facilitates that process and brings a fresh perspective that can be particularly valuable for a singer-songwriter. Here's how Jerry Douglas described the back and forth between producer and artist in the preproduction phase.

> *Normally what you're doing is going through a bunch of songs, and something might strike me that they didn't hear or the other way around. If they don't write a lot, you might want to get them fired up to write more or get them excited about their writing and improving their writing.*
>
> *When I used to do Tim O'Brien's records, he would come out with this big armload of songs and he'd say, "These are all terrible." He lived with the songs, and he didn't really get outside of himself with the songs sometimes. They were incredibly deep songs, and we just shaped them and gave them arrangements that made them hold together and instrumental parts that helped even more to tell the story. And then they started to look like something. He would be happy—he would laugh out loud, "I didn't know this was in the song!"*
>
> —Jerry Douglas

Beyond helping to improve individual songs, a producer might also have a clear idea of the whole album and how to give it a distinct identity. As the artist, you are on the long road of writing, playing, recording, and developing, and it's harder for you to see this one project as separate from everything else you do. A producer zeroes right in on the impression that this particular recording will make.

If I'm falling in love with the songs, I can usually get a pretty good idea of what the record will sound like right away.
—Gurf Morlix

❖ ***Take care of business.*** Along with doing the conceptual and creative work, the producer deals with such unsexy things as budgets, deadlines, and label input. On a simple project with a small label, these administrative matters might not add up to much, but every little detail you have to take care of is a potential distraction from making the music.

❖ ***Hire the supporting cast.*** Unless he or she doubles as an engineer, the producer brings in the engineer(s), who may or may not come attached to a studio. Many producers have engineers they work with regularly and rely on for particular types of sounds, which is good because you're getting a team with a (literal) track record.

Unless you have a regular band or are going solo, the producer also assembles whatever session players are needed to bring to life the record you're collectively imagining. Even if you do have a band, sometimes a producer needs to gently suggest that the drummer sit out a particular song, or that bringing in a pedal steel player would be cooler than having the guitar solo that usually happens. Better that someone else make that sort of comment and judgment than you.

❖ ***Direct the recording process.*** A producer may rely on an engineer to oversee the technical details of the recording process, but he or she will at least lay out the basics of where and how the record is going to be made and what sort of platform is going to capture it. That includes the critical question of how you and the other musicians will be set up (playing together in the same room, playing together but separated, building the song track by track, or some combination of the above).

❖ *Cheerlead.* Great records begin with great performances, and a producer does whatever it takes to make them happen. That means getting everyone jazzed about the material and then setting the right vibe in the studio, so all the players feel relaxed and confident. It means being diplomatic and encouraging, and knowing when to actively direct and when to just get out of the way. As T Bone Burnett suggested, it might mean making tea at the appropriate moment. (Patrick Simmons of the Doobie Brothers told me that the producers of the band's early albums believed that alcohol fueled their best tracks, so he was duly supplied with Southern Comfort along with his guitar when recording solo pieces. That's an anecdote, not a recommendation.)

A good producer is your ally in the studio, someone who recognizes your strengths and knows how to work with and—ultimately—help you stretch beyond what you thought you could do. When the producer/artist chemistry is right, it transforms the process of record making and even songwriting. Chris Whitley once described how during a dark period when "I didn't have the confidence to even know whether I could stand what I was writing," renowned producer Craig Street (Cassandra Wilson, k.d. lang) helped him believe in his songs again and keep the new material flowing. Even though the record they made at the time (*Dirt Floor*) wasn't "produced" at all—it was recorded in one day in a barn, live and solo—Street had played a central role in making it possible.

So, given this general job description for a producer, should you produce your own record? Malcolm Burn's advice is crystal clear.

Don't. There's a reason why producers have their jobs, and it's not because they are money-sucking leeches. It's because they bring something to a project which can only be gained by experience and knowledge and good taste and maybe a great record collection. You still need some people around who have that experi-

ence—to know when a good idea is a good idea, to know when a bad idea is just not worth pursuing, to know what a great sound really sounds like and how to get it.

I think if you can afford a producer, you should have one. Self-production is probably not a great idea, especially if you're in a band and want the band to be around awhile. You need somebody there to field the questions, to be the middleman, to do all the things that nobody else wants to do.

—Malcolm Burn

Not everyone agrees with that assessment of self-production: some musicians love having complete control over the process, and they feel that a producer is an unnecessary intermediary who dilutes their ideas. But even for these determined do-it-yourselfers, there are essential helpers behind the scenes—at the very least, an engineer, band member, session player, manager, or friend who can act as a sounding board. If you really try to go it alone as singer/songwriter/player/engineer/producer, you risk getting lost in a house of mirrors, where you're overwhelmed by all the reflections and don't know which is your true face anymore.

It's really hard to sit there in your home studio and make a record and be sure that it sounds like you want it to sound. You need another person to bounce things off of. Everyone who produces their own records has got one. They've got somebody else around and they can go, "Listen to this. Give me your honest opinion. Have I gone over the top with this?" Or "Am I loud enough?" A lot of people who produce their own records will not mix themselves loud enough.

—Jerry Douglas

If you're seeking engineering or production help for a recording project, be sure to ask candidates for other work they've done. If none of their sample recordings sounds remotely like what you want to do, keep looking. You want proof, not promises, of what they can deliver. The whole process will be much smoother and quicker if they normally work with music and production values similar to your project and you can agree on specific recordings as a reference point.

Pay attention, too, to your gut feeling about what it would be like to hole up with a particular person for hours or days and share the intimate process of creating music. Will you feel comfortable, respected, free to speak your mind, ready to take chances? Or might the situation turn out to be awkward and tense? For good or bad, the mood that pervades the studio will be memorialized in your recorded songs.

MAKING TRACKS

The recording studio these days is a perfectionist's paradise. A song can be assembled piece by piece on virtually unlimited tracks, and then each individual sound can be edited at a microscopic level of detail. Real-time performances become waveforms on a screen that can be cut, pasted, altered, combined, and repaired ad infinitum. Even on an inexpensive home-recording box, wizardly powers are at your fingertips, and it's easy to get swept away in the creative and technological possibilities.

As intoxicating as the process of using these tools can be, what you have to remember is that in the end the process doesn't matter. Listeners respond to your final mix, and they won't know or care how you got there; what they care about is how the words and music make them *feel*. In the studio, you have to take off your wizard's hat and put yourself in the position of those listeners, hearing the song for the first time. At every turn in the recording process you need to ask yourself, "Am I enhancing their experience or just doing cool studio stuff because I can?" And, by extension, "Am I giving my own song the treatment it deserves?"

In recording, as in all musical pursuits, what works for one individual would be ineffective or inadvisable for another. Through experimentation and experience, artists learn how to coax the best music out of themselves in the studio, and how to translate those moments into a stream of data that will come alive for someone hearing it through car speakers or the home stereo or headphones at the gym. It's an ongoing quest—at the end of every recording session, it seems, comes a scheme for how to do things a little differently next time. Here are some tips and tactics to use in your ventures behind the studio glass.

❖ *Watch the interplay of your instrument and voice.* As a singer-songwriter, you have developed a subtle and sophisticated partnership between your vocal and instrumental styles. When you're singing, you adapt your playing to better support your voice and stay out of its way; and when you are playing, you sing differently than you would if your hands had no job to do but hold the microphone or make photogenic gestures. These adaptations are largely unconscious—you don't really notice how much the two functions influence each other until you try to separate them in the studio, as engineers often like to do so there's no bleed between vocal and instrument mics.

> *When I separate the voice from the guitar, to come back and do a voice track, I begin to intellectualize and think, "How should I sing this?" When I play guitar I'm not analyzing.*
>
> —Patty Larkin

Whenever I try to do separate vocal and instrument tracks, I find that my backup parts suffer the most. The groove is weaker, and my playing tends to be too busy—I'm not giving the vocal enough breathing room. Like Patty Larkin, I get self-conscious in a way that I never do when the vocal is demanding my full attention. The whole setup—doing the rhythm part while running through verses in my head—just feels artificial.

The same considerations apply to a session in which you are singing over other people's backup: pay attention to what happens when you sing separately from your core accompaniment.

My first record was live, but it was solo. And the second record, the band recorded while I was in the control room, and then I would do separate days of vocals where I would listen to the band on my headphones. And it didn't work for me. It made me sing careful and cautious—not to mention there's no audience, I am in a quiet room, and it's really loud in my ears. It was just different.

—Jewel

❖ *Be spontaneous.* If everything on your record is thoroughly planned out, labored over, and polished to a high gloss, it will sound that way. Music gets a charge of energy from accidents and ideas that emerge (or combust) in the moment; that's what makes it sound like humans having fun playing songs rather than a computer spooling out rows of code. So crack open the studio door to serendipity; as Beck once said, the moment when the pizza delivery guy interrupts your session could be the best part of the track.

If you are building a song instrument by instrument, you can still inject spontaneity into the proceedings—in fact, when you're doing a lot of overdubs it's especially important to loosen up so the music has that elusive live feel.

You have to pay attention to it the whole time so you don't lose it. Part of it is being spontaneous when you're overdubbing: over-dubbing inside the control room where the mic is picking up what's coming off the speakers, things that enhance a live feel to the tracks that you're putting down on top of everything. And then not getting so precious on every little thing really helps.

—Amy Ray

It sounds paradoxical, but there are ways in which you can plan to be spontaneous in the studio. Nickel Creek's Chris Thile told me about a clever tactic that producer Alison Krauss used while he was overdubbing vocal harmonies. On the band's mischievous cover of Carrie Newcomer's "I Should've Known Better," Krauss had Thile improvise harmony part after harmony part while listening to the lead vocal. She never played back the parts he had already record-ed—she just asked for another and another and another, bang bang

Jewel

bang. When they finally did audition all those parts together, there were strange and evocative cluster harmonies, with the various lines moving around, across, and sometimes against each other—the kind of thing that could only come about by accident, and a brilliant match for the off-kilter feel of that track.

❖ *Leave the bark on it.* That's Jerry Douglas' phrase for not fussing all the life out of the music. There's a difference between a mistake that jumps out and draws attention, and a little blip of not-quite-perfect playing or phrasing that nobody else but you is ever going to notice. It's much easier to distinguish between a fatal flaw and a harmless lapse in somebody else's performance than it is in your own, so gather some additional opinions before you decide how to proceed.

In considering whether to fix a mistake, you have to weigh what will be gained (one place in the song that you can now listen to without grimacing) versus what might be lost (the organic feel of that section). Remember that the bark is what makes a tree look like a tree—and keeps it healthy and alive. Cut off the dead limbs if you like, but leave the bark.

❖ *Listen to the logic.* When you perform a song from beginning to end, there is a natural logic to the way your take unfolds. Phrase B sounds like it does because of the way you played Phrase A; Phrase C builds on an idea you happened upon in Phrase B, and then Phrase D brings it to a conclusion. A slightly garbled word on one chorus leads you to emphatically declare it on the next repetition. Stretching for that high note on the bridge makes your voice a tad hoarse early in the next verse. All these little connections are what make that rendition of the song a unified performance.

With the powerful editing tools available today, you have to pay close attention to this chain of action and reaction. Unless you want a jarring cross-cut effect, avoid cutting and pasting things together that just do not follow each other because they are divorced from the context in which they made perfect sense. The same problem can arise when you go back to change something in a track that you recorded at another time: when you first did the track maybe you were completely wired from that double espresso and cinnamon bun, and today you're feeling much mellower and so will have a hard time matching the mood and feel of the original.

If you are unhappy with a few sections of a track that you generally like, sometimes it makes more sense to do the entire thing again so you get a second performance that's cohesive and has that internal logic.

> For me the stage is an immediate, visceral, highly exposed, vulnerable place, and making a record is kind of vicarious. . . . The fact that there's no audience in the studio is a hurdle for me to begin with. I just can't sit around and try to make the perfect vocal and the perfect guitar track. I lose artistic inspiration for that kind of obsessiveness. So what I've learned to do is to record a bunch of different times, because the song as you play it on any given day is just that day's interpretation. I thought, "OK, if I can't sit for a week and think about a song in the studio and play it a hundred times, then maybe I could record a bunch of songs this week, record all those same songs four months later, somewhere else, and then do it again three months later." Then you have a few different versions that happen in the moment, but you can put them against each other and say, "OK, this one sounds most like the song, and that one, I don't know what we were on that day."
> —Ani DiFranco

❖ *Use that first-take feel.* There's always something special about the first take, when you're rekindling your relationship with a piece of music. Don't squander that moment by playing the song all the way through while warming up or testing levels. Save your first real, full-throttle performance for when the gear is ready, because subsequent takes may not have the same spark.

As Ani DiFranco suggested, you can capture multiple first takes if you allow for rest time in between. That can be a good alternative to bludgeoning a song over and over until you can barely stand to play the opening chords.

Ani DiFranco

❖ *Try it live.* If a live ensemble feel is what you are seeking, the sometimes overlooked or overruled way to achieve it is to play that way. Never mind the crowded room with all the wires to trip over, or the difficulty of fixing mistakes because everyone is bleeding onto everyone else's track. The gain in energy and synchronicity might more than offset the loss in technical control. Just as there's a logic to a solo performance, in a band performance there's a dynamic give and take between the musicians that doesn't happen in the same way when the parts are being overdubbed.

> What a difference to listen to a track and then just go into a room by yourself and play along with the track, versus going into a room with four awesome people and having eye contact and playing off of each other. It's entirely different. Granted, record making and live playing are different crafts, but it doesn't seem to me as though they can't cross here and there.
>
> —Alana Davis

❖ *Get in a band state of mind.* Of course, recording the band live isn't always possible or even preferable. When you are overdubbing individual parts, don't forget that you still *are* a member of the band. Those are people playing in your headphones, not just static tracks. Close your eyes and lose yourself in the flow of sound.

> Being your own band ... sure, it's hard. But why not grow, why not learn how to do it with feeling and make it sound like it's live? Because if it's living in you at that time then it *is* live, even though it's not happening at the same time. What is the difference between me sitting in here and another guy in there, playing on two different tracks, and me playing one part and then going in there? If you can really lock in on the tape, it's your mind that makes it live.
>
> —Michael Hedges

❖ **_Beware the click._** One way that studios facilitate the piece-by-piece recording of a song is through the use of a click track—the electronic metronome ticking in everyone's headphones that keeps them on time. The click is a huge help for getting rhythm tracks in sync, and the rock-steady beat is at the core of lots of music. But don't lose sight of what happens when you make your own time: you get excited and speed up, you slow down as you approach the ending, you extend a pause a little just because it feels good. The primal pulse of music is more like the heartbeat than the metronome. So be conscious of how you are using the beat, and make sure you're letting the song find its own sweet time.

❖ **_Get some distance._** In recording, you often need a little mental and physical distance to judge the results. Songs will sound very different at another time and another place and on a different set of audio equipment. So after you have listened to your freshly made tracks in the studio, come back the next day and see if they strike you the same way. Take a tape home and hear how it sounds on your stereo. Spin it in your car. Play it at a low volume and listen from the next room, or while you are doing the dishes, and take note of which elements you can hear. Are the most important things (e.g., your voice) coming through? Try the same exercise with one of your favorite CDs—is the balance very different from the balance on your songs?

Although it would be nice if everyone listened to our recordings through gleaming audiophile sound systems in acoustically optimized rooms that are otherwise silent, the world just isn't like that. That's why pop producers who work in big-budget studios take tapes out to their cars or play them through cheap speakers as a final test. If the music sounds good there, it'll stand up anywhere.

❖ **_Get a second opinion._** As we discussed in the section on producers and engineers, it's essential for those working on their own to use another person as a sounding board. You start off with a clear idea of what you're trying to achieve, but deep into the process you might find yourself wondering if you're heading in the right direction or if your original idea was totally misguided. The quickest way to break out of this maze of uncertainty and self-doubt is to get a second opinion from someone whose taste and honesty you trust. Even if you don't take their advice, an opposing view can help clarify where you stand.

❖ *Subtract as well as add.* With all those empty tracks laid out in front of you, it is always tempting to add sounds. And add. And add some more. Go ahead—pull out the didgeridoo for the intro or sing your tenth harmony part. But be sure to listen back to see if you've really added something or are just filling space. It's always a good exercise to put all the faders down to zero, then bring the tracks in slowly, one by one, starting with the most important ones—probably the vocal and main rhythm parts. You might be surprised to discover that what seemed essential doesn't really contribute that much to the mix.

> You don't have to make records that are complete structures. You can let people guess at what the other stuff might be, use their imagination for what might be there. It's great sometimes when you think you hear something in a piece of recorded music, but it's just your brain filling in what you want to be there at a particular point of time. To me, that's always a good point to stop.
>
> —Craig Street

❖ *Be a songwriter, then a recording artist.* The most important preparation you can do for a recording project isn't shopping for new equipment, reading recording magazines, or even making practice tapes; it's working on your songs. When you've really put heart and soul into the writing and come up with your best material, the recording process is so much simpler. You're not trying to use studio tricks to manufacture excitement and intrigue in a track; you're spotlighting the excitement and intrigue that's already built into the writing. Your job in the studio becomes so much clearer, and the gear so much less important.

> *People are now so consumed by technology, and there's so much of it available, but the only thing that really differentiates one person from another is who's got the best ideas and the most interesting musical concepts. I'm not interested in who's got the coolest microphone and the best mixing board or whatever it is they've got. At the end of the day, there's no substitute for great ideas.*
> —Malcolm Burn

The Label Connection

Let's step out of the studio now and consider how your spanking new recording might make its way into listeners' hands. What are the pros and cons of going the do-it-yourself record company route? What do traditional labels have to offer? How about a small independent label versus a larger indie versus a major?

The most compelling reason to be your own record label is control. You decide what sort of record to make and when to release it. You decide how it's packaged, how it's publicized, and how you want to sell it or give it away. Unlike most artists in the history of the record business, you own the master recordings that you make and the songs that you write, rather than having signed them over to a company that has its own agenda and short-term interests. You are in charge of your own destiny—both creative and financial.

> *Record companies are always looking to jump on a trend and give it a modern sound, but the things that make it sound modern now will make it sound dated in a few years. My back catalog is quite*

valuable to me, and albums I did five years ago still sell quite well. I spend most of my life building a new audience, and my entire catalog is new to my new audience. Because I'm in a field where I'm not doing trend-oriented stuff—in fact I've consciously steered away from that—an album of me just playing solo guitar is going to sound the same in 30 years as it does now.

—Harvey Reid

If you create it, you're not going to wait around for some big company to sign you to a label. You don't wait around for these people to acknowledge you. Meanwhile, sure, you make less, you learn to live cheap, you really learn to find your wants and needs in a sensible fashion. But, at a subindustrial level, you make all the artistic decisions—not the people in the front office, not the people who try to shape your image—and that's what keeps the material flowing and fresh. When you give in to their system, when you become a bought person and they're going to give you wealth, power, and fame, and the creative decisions are then being made more and more by the people in the front office, all you can begin to write about is your personal sense of alienation.

—Utah Phillips

The downside of being in charge is that, well, you are in charge. You have to hire and pay the large cast of characters involved in making a record: the studio, the players, the recording and mastering engineers, the photographer, the graphic designer, the printer and duplicator . . . All these expenses add up fast, so you either need to make a substantial investment yourself or find somebody else who wants to back you—and you will probably have to scale down your ambitions considerably (a string section would be really cool on that one song, but maybe next time). And along with paying for everything, you have to *do* everything yourself or oversee the work of others who are helping you. If you are acting as your own publisher, you have to affiliate yourself with a performance rights society, register a fictitious business name (the procedures vary by state), and copyright the songs; if your CD includes covers of other people's copyrighted songs, you have to get mechanical licenses and then track and pay royalties; and you need to copyright your recording itself (see Resources for suggestions on where to learn more about these aspects of the business). And then you have to figure out how you're going to distribute the CD . . . Handling all these administrative matters is a big job, which is why many artists find a partner for running their labels— a manager is a natural choice.

> I think a lot of people have this impression that I'm a colossal control freak, that I have to do everything myself. But once you make the decision that you're not going to work for a corporation and you still want to make music, there's nobody else around to do all of that stuff, and for years I've coveted the help of, for instance, a graphic designer. It's only recently that I've had the money to pay people or the phone number to call when I need help of a certain sort.
>
> —Ani DiFranco

When you put out a CD yourself, you also become the sales force behind it. You're not relying on singles, advertising, videos, and retail promotion to stoke up the demand for your disc. Your primary sales tool is getting your butt up in front of people and playing your songs so well that they just have to buy your CD after the show (and then tell their friends to buy it too). Thanks to the Web and the many e-commerce sites catering to independent musicians, you can have global distribution in theory, but in reality the odds of selling your CD to a random Internet surfer are mighty slim and getting slimmer all the time just because of the bazillions of other sites out there; the Web functions mostly as a very handy place where people who have heard you or heard about you can track you down and see, hear, and read more. You sell fewer copies with this person-to-person approach than you might with mass marketing, but because your operation is so lean and you have no middleman, you keep a much higher percentage of the money that does come in.

I remember years ago when I was working with Warners, our agreement was that I could buy my stuff at cost and sell it on the road, those kind of places. Well, their cost was twice as much as what I actually had to pay to manufacture it myself. I said, "How is that?" And they said, "Well, we have big buildings filled with secre-

Arlo Guthrie

taries and limousines and lunches and stuff like that." I didn't have any of that, so the cost of me doing it … it didn't make sense to go with a large label, especially nowadays with the Internet and people can buy and trade and listen to stuff whenever they want worldwide.

—Arlo Guthrie

One rung up the record-business ladder are small independent labels, run on shoestring budgets by people who love the music (if they didn't, they—like you—would find a more sensible way to make a living). When you sign with a small indie label, you get help with the promotional and administrative matters mentioned above, plus some financial support for making the record and possibly for going on tour to promote it; in return, you are sharing a portion of the revenues. A good label has the kind of relationships with press, radio, retail, and distributors that are very hard or impossible to develop when you're putting out release number 001—or even 006—on your own label. The imprint of an established label gives your CD credibility in the business as well as with consumers. If the label is doing its job (and that's always a big *if*), your CD's odds of getting into stores, getting reviews, and getting noticed at all are higher than if you were handling these areas yourself.

The main advantage of working with a label is in the marketing and visibility of your CD. We obviously have more resources and invest more in publicity, advertising, radio campaigns, and such—things that are hard to do as an independent artist, especially if you're starting from scratch. And also being part of a roster of other artists, I think, helps to establish who you are and what your music is about. It puts you in a subset of artists. We've tried to put together the sort of roster where if you like the music of one of our artists, you are more than likely to like the others. We are trying to get a level of consistency.

—Jim Olsen

One possible advantage of working with a small label rather than a large indie or a major label is flexibility in your contract. Especially if you've built a track record and audience on your own, you stand a better chance of negotiating a deal in which you own your masters outright and license them to the record company, or the label owns the record but all rights revert to you if it's no longer available in retail channels or if the company goes under. Maybe you can hold on to your publishing—the ownership and control of your song copyrights—an extremely important deal point for a singer-songwriter (more on that below). The details of an agreement like this are significant down to the last *hereinafter* and percentage point, so don't take chances: get a good lawyer to vet any contract before you sign it (not just record deals but agreements with agents, managers, etc.), no matter how much you trust and like the people you're going to do business with.

You shouldn't expect a small label, with its limited staff and finances, to turn your record into a runaway hit. A well-run indie can build on what you have accomplished on your own and help you step up to the next level, but it can't create that coveted thing called buzz out of silence. Even tiny labels are looking for artists who have already made some headway in the business—selling their own records and, especially, touring actively and widely.

I advise artists to think about it from a label's perspective: How can a label sell my CDs? You can't rely on big radio play, because that is locked up by the major labels, who participate in payola-like schemes. Articles in the press help but do not sell lots of records. Therefore, artists need to tour and play in front of real people and make a concerted effort on their own to build a following. We work extremely hard for our bands, but we expect them to be doing the same.

—Brandon Kessler

Bigger independent labels have more money, more staff, better distribution, and correspondingly bigger catalogs to administer. The line is sometimes blurry between the largest indies and the major labels—some indies are distributed through the majors, and major labels have also bought up prominent indies and let them operate more or less autonomously in order to take advantage of their counterculture image and ear-to-the-ground intelligence about new music. In recent years, indie labels have also signed quite a few well-known pop/rock artists who've fallen from grace at the majors, so indies are more than ever working the stylistic mainstream.

From the artist's standpoint, dealing with a large and high-profile company can be a plus or a minus. It's nice that there is a team of publicists rather than just one, but are they dealing with so many releases each month that they are just turning the crank? If a former chart topper is your label mate, does that enhance your visibility or just steal the label's attention away from your record?

Independent labels pride themselves on having interests beyond the bottom line, but they still have rent and salaries to pay each month. The most stable and successful companies tend to have a handful of artists who sell enough records to bankroll the rest. The same is true of major labels—superstars generate the lion's share of profits. The difference is that an indie might keep the lesser known acts on the roster out of a sense of responsibility to the music, while the major will drop them as fast as they can.

They decide pretty quick if you're not going to be one of the few acts that pays the bills for all the other ones. If after three weeks your record isn't headed for platinum, they kind of lose interest.

—Dan Bern

Where major labels excel is in working with the records that *are* headed for platinum. They know how to milk that moment for all it is worth. Mass marketing and mass distribution are their forte, and music with a "cult" following is an uneasy and temporary fit.

Music-business cynics (and they are an ever-growing tribe) like to depict the major labels as masterminding some kind of evil conspiracy to force-feed cheesy music to the world. The reality, I think, is far less colorful and James Bond–esque than that. As with all big businesses, it's about the numbers. Major labels are happy to give free creative rein to artists who consistently make blockbuster records. If Renaissance lute music was suddenly selling millions of records, the major labels would dispatch all their A&R people to early-music programs to sign the next big star. We'd have videos of lutenists with gyrating dancers and smoke machines at their feet. The soft-drink ads and movie tie-ins would quickly follow. As long as recordings of Francesco da Milano's fantasias kept selling in big numbers, the labels would keep churning them out—and eventually the stores and airwaves would be saturated with the work of glamorous-looking, marginally talented lutenists. As soon as the numbers started to fall, all those lute slingers would be back on their own, and the labels would start sniffing around for the next big thing.

> *If you're great and you're a genius and you've really got something, you'll probably hit it big at some point and then you'll fade into obscurity because that's what the music business does. It's all based on the premise that it's got to be today's thing, and of course you can't be today's thing tomorrow, so you'll be yesterday's thing. You'll be out the door no matter who you are. You could be the Marx Brothers, Buck Owens, Elvis Presley. Tomorrow they'll be selling something else, so you'll be in the cutout bin, no matter if you sold three records or if you sold 300 million records.*
>
> *Then, if you survive for another seven, eight, ten, or twelve years, you'll be rediscovered, because people, having not been able to think of anything new during those years, will gravitate back to the shit that they grew up listening to, and they'll start copying*

that. And then maybe, if you had a big enough influence, they'll come around and find you because you're still great at that and you originated it. So they'll just rediscover you and put your name out there again. And if you live long enough you could do this three or four times.

—David Grisman

On that curmudgeonly note, let's turn to the pertinent question: Where do you and your record fit into this industry picture?

When you're just starting out, the clear (and, for most artists, the only) choice is to put out your music yourself. It's the best way to get your bearings in the studio and in the record business, and it gives you something to sell at gigs and over the Web and to use for promotion. Releasing your own CD gives you a quick sense of whether the do-it-yourself approach suits you or not, which will help you plot out your next career moves. Even if your ultimate goal is to sign with a label, a little DIY success will give you leverage and know-how when you do go shopping for a record deal.

When you've built enough of an audience and reputation that a label is interested in putting out your records, you still need to weigh what this company might be able to do for you versus what you can do for yourself. Will you get significant publicity support when the record comes out and while you're out on tour? Will the record be available and visible beyond your gigs and your Web site? Are there opportunities for shared bills and industry showcases with other artists on the label? And what sort of funds will be available for making the record in the first place?

If you make a record that is bare bones, that is the singer-songwriter and maybe a couple other instruments and is basically about the songs—it's not about the production—then you'll probably sell it at a limited number of places: at your own gigs, at Amazon.com. You're probably not going to do much marketing of it, and it probably won't get to radio. If it's sort of a representation of your live thing, a keepsake or something like that, do it yourself absolutely. What's the point of turning that over to a record company?

Much of it is about initial financing. It seems to me that if you can fund an album without really compromising your own craft in the process, and you can fund the marketing of it yourself, then you are better off doing it yourself, because then you are going to end up owning a master and you are in control of your destiny. But if you don't have that kind of funding, and there is a company that totally believes in you and thinks that they are really going to help build your career and make you a priority and do the right kind of marketing and sales positioning—and especially if they are going to help with tour support—then you are better off being with a company.
—Dawn Atkinson

It's tricky to compare the economics of an artist label versus an indie versus a major label, because they operate at completely different scales. You can make an inexpensive record, sell it on your own label in small numbers through limited channels, and promote it through low-budget solo touring—that can be a sustainable (though not necessarily lucrative) enterprise, because the expenses and revenues are in scale with each other. If you want to make a more complicated band record, you need to invest more up front and then sell more records to recoup the investment; more sales means in turn that you'll need to spend more on promotion; and if you want to take that awesome band on the road to showcase the record, you have to be playing bigger halls in order to pay and feed everyone, or else you have to subsidize the road work as a promotional expense (plus you'll need an agent who can get you booked in those halls in the first place). At that level of the business, the resources of a label become very attractive, if not essential. At a major label, the investment in production and marketing ratchets up so far (into hundreds of thousands of dollars to try to break a song on the radio) that only a serious hit is going to pay off.

If you sell five or six or even seven hundred thousand, that's kind of the low end of success for a major label. You are pretty much in danger of being dropped even if you sell that many, which for someone like me would be winning the lottery. So when you go into it independently, your whole plan is based on a completely different reality. You have to rewrite your success program and say, "Wait, what really is success and what's not? What will constitute enough? What will constitute satisfaction and a sense of having done really everything I could?"

—Jonatha Brooke

The different scales of the industry explain why a gold-selling artist on a major label might be in debt and in danger of career crash-and-burn, while a troubadour who fills folk clubs with devoted CD-buying fans might be able to make a steady, although not

Jonatha Brooke

cushy, living over the long term. In purely economic terms, you have to consider any potential record deal in light of the question: Which is bigger, a small slice of a big pie or a big slice of a small pie? The answer depends on the relative sizes of the slices and of the pies.

You're making a record that you hope will still be attractive and saleable years from now, so you also need to think about what happens with the finances in the long run. And that's where ownership of the master recording and the songs themselves is so important.

I look at my copyrights as my retirement fund.

—Harvey Reid

Don't give your publishing away. Realize the value of your publishing. A lot of times what these labels are doing is throwing the publishing [into the contract], thinking that no one is going to question it because these younger or somewhat smaller artists are so happy to be getting a record deal that they don't want to rock the boat. They think that if they question the contract in terms of something major like publishing, they might scare the record label away.

The initial draft of a contract is usually the most onerous, and you should try to negotiate down from it. They expect to be negotiated with. You need to assess your bargaining position, of course. If they're doing you a favor and you go in and say, "Well, this change and this change and this change," they might come back and say, "Absolutely not. If you want this change, then that's a deal breaker." But at least by negotiating you've gotten to the point where you realize what they really want.

I would try to eliminate publishing entirely from the record deal. Sometimes you can't do that—sometimes the label is only interested in signing you if they can get you as an artist and as a songwriter. If you can't knock it out entirely, then try to limit it as much as possible. The best way to do that is after a set number of years the copyrights will revert to you, and if you do work out some sort of situation like that, be sure that the language in the agreement is very clear that it reverts on a certain date and that it reverts without further formalities, because you don't want to have to go to them and put them on notice and send a letter. You can get into a battle with the record label because they won't want to write a letter or they will take their sweet time doing it. So make sure that the reversion is clean and easy—that's a big thing.

—Kyle Staggs

No matter how you make your way through the tangle of the record business, remember that in the end everything comes back to you and your music. All a label can do is to brighten the spotlight on you and amplify the excitement that you're generating with audiences. The things that keep a DIY career going—gigs, an active Web presence, a substantial mailing list, record sales direct to fans—are actually the same things that a label would look for in considering you for the roster.

You often hear this phrase: "Distribution is the key." It's not a key to anything, unless you have a lot of people looking for your disc. Your disc can be in every Tower Records in America, and nobody will buy it by accident. You have to create the demand.

—Andrew Calhoun

SURVIVING AND THRIVING IN THE DIY AGE

Throughout these pages we've talked about the opportunities and challenges of taking the music, and the business behind it, into your own hands—from writing and performing your own songs and being your own song editor to booking yourself and producing, releasing, and promoting your own records. As the boss and chief labor force of your own cottage industry, you will find that the list of additional jobs you might take on keeps going: publicist, publisher, Webmaster, manager, roadie, sound crew, merchandiser . . . Many artists shoulder all these roles out of necessity rather than choice, yet there is an appealing kind of purity about music that is written, played, and presented by a single hand. There is no filter between the creator and the listener.

The conceptual appeal of DIY doesn't change the fact that it is very tough to manage all of these tasks yourself while creating the music. You didn't become a singer-songwriter to fulfill your dream of being a mailing-list administrator or a virtuoso with the photocopy machine. You might find it interesting and challenging to learn everything there is to know about mechanical licensing or color separations, but there's always the danger that all this business and technical detail will steal too much attention away from the songs. If the day-to-day operation of DIY, Inc., starts to overshadow the art, what's the point of running the company in the first place? As Ani DiFranco once wrote in an open letter to the editors of *Ms.* magazine, "If I drop dead tomorrow, tell me my gravestone won't read: ani d. / CEO. Please let it read: songwriter / music maker / storyteller / freak."

Cultivating your creative life while attending to your career is a big challenge and a preoccupation of all independent artists. Let's close this tour of the singer-songwriter world with some reflections on how to maintain that elusive balance between making the music and making a living.

❖ ***Look on the bright side.*** When you're feeling bogged down by making yet more copies of your bio to put in promo packs to take to the post office and send to people who might not give them a second glance—this is a good time to play a little game called Consider the Alternative. Every job has its tedious, annoying, or unsatisfying aspects; at least you are trying to facilitate something deeply gratifying and meaningful rather than devoting yourself to selling widgets. There really are worse things you could be doing with your time (just flip through the newspaper classifieds if you need a reminder).

> You can't play guitar all day long—you get tendinitis. You've got to do something else. If you spend a lot of time on the phone, mailing things, or Xeroxing things—the business part of it—when it's time to play music, it's real fresh.
>
> —Harvey Reid

❖ ***Learn to delegate.*** As has been suggested numerous times in this book, for many of the jobs that need to be done, you are better off knuckling down and doing them yourself—like booking your gigs when you're starting out or releasing your first CD. But you can go too far with self-reliance and drive yourself batty. So make it your mission to learn not only how to do things yourself but how to delegate—and then to refrain from micromanaging your helpers, which is both annoying to them and extra work for you. Beware the control-freak syndrome, in which you reluctantly pass a job along to someone else, constantly look over his shoulder and "correct" what he is doing, and then decide (with secret satisfaction) that since you just *have* to supervise so closely to make sure he's doing it right, you're better off just doing it yourself. There are some jobs that nobody else can do as well as you can (like writing *your* songs!), but the world is full of smart and capable people. Find them and hire them.

> A mistake I made when I was just starting out was to try to do everything myself. While I am certainly a better businesswoman for understanding how the industry works, I neglected my creative life in the process. You have to have help—so find some good help and trust them. You can't ever completely check out of the business side of your career (which I have also done at times to devastating effect), but you can definitely find a way to supervise without devoting all your time to it. It is a certain skill in itself to recognize someone who can help you, but if you never try it . . . you'll just be sitting in Kinko's a lot.
>
> In general, I try to keep my business work confined to my computer and a couple days a week. Obviously if things are jumping that isn't always possible, but I try anyway. I have a room at home that I write in, where all my instruments and my four-track (I am a fanatic four-tracker!) are ready to go. When I am not on tour, I really focus on being in that room for a little time every day and just trying to do something. I also keep a notebook with me always—somehow it makes me feel like a writer, and feeling like a writer is the fastest way to becoming one. I find I have to be really vigilant

about this; spending enough time on my art is one of the areas in which I need the greatest improvement. It is so easy to move information around and so difficult to generate new ideas, but a new song solves all your problems quickly!

—Erin McKeown

❖ ***Enlist your fans.*** Not all your help has to be paid help. Your fan base—however humble—is a pool of potential volunteers for the cause of your music. People who discover and love the music of an emerging independent artist are particularly passionate and loyal—they feel like they have a stake in your success. Encourage them to get involved and you'll both be happy and rewarded.

You do need to be careful about assigning significant responsibilities to well-meaning but inexperienced volunteers. As mentioned in the discussion of booking, it's not a good idea to ask someone like this to be your main contact with venues, but he or she might be able to help gather information that you can follow up with. Publicity involves compiling lists, doing mailings, and following up by phone and e-mail in an organized fashion—tasks you can train someone else to do. And who better to promote your virtues than a diehard fan?

Many artists effectively use their Web sites to recruit street teams who help promote a new record or concert in their city. In return for show tickets or T-shirts or some other perk, the fans put up posters (you can e-mail the layout for them to print out), contact local radio and press, and round up people to go to a show. Some small labels use volunteers located via e-mail lists and chat rooms to check the stock in local record stores and offer posters and display copies of CDs. These relationships are invaluable and help to compensate for an independent musician's lack of marketing resources.

Think creatively about what fans might be able to do for you, and—especially—what they would enjoy doing. Ask e-mail list subscribers and visitors to your Web site if they're interested in hosting a house concert, for instance, and then help prospective hosts figure out how to do one (see Resources). As an alternative to shopping for a label, some established artists get fans to help finance a record by preordering it or making a loan up front (be very cautious about taking people's money, though, and hyper clear about what's expected of them and of you). For the converted, it's a thrill to play any kind of part in the creation and propagation of good music.

❖ *Call a specialist.* Aside from the ever-present clerical and grunt work, some aspects of the music business require a great deal of training and brain cells to master. Hiring a specialist can give you both peace of mind and precious time to do something else. You can have an entertainment lawyer, for instance, vet a contract for

Erin McKeown

you and explain what all that impenetrable jargon means (just make sure you keep a lid on the billable hours!). Not only will that get you a more favorable contract, but the lawyer spares you having to be the hardball negotiator with people (like agents or managers) you want to treat as your friends and allies. Another example is music publishing: you can own your songs but sign with a company for publishing administration, which can become dauntingly complex when it comes to collaboration, licensing for film and TV, and international business.

> *If you think you can pull it off, and you want to spend your day chasing after money in Switzerland on a record that you had a song on, well then, great. But if you can get somebody for 10 percent of what you are making to do that for you, I think it's well worth it. Go write another song—that's how I look at it.*
>
> *—Steve Seskin*

❖ ***Separate the marketing from the creating.*** A perennial issue for songwriters is how to categorize the music they make. All manner of sounds, styles, and ideas are swirling around in the air, and each writer takes a little from here and a little from there to create something new and, in essence, uncategorizable. But the marketplace requires that music be labeled in some way, so it fits into a bin in the record store or a format at the radio station or a particular type of performance venue. And that categorizing may have as much to do with how you dress or where you come from as what the songs sound like. Guitar-toting troubadours, for instance, are typically put in the folk bin regardless of what their influences and intentions are.

It's a marketing game, and you have to play it somehow if you are going to try to sell records and play gigs. So, as we noted earlier in the book, find a simple and catchy way to label your music rather than let someone else do it. But don't let the barriers between styles and genres dictate the kind of music you make.

There are creative barriers and mechanical (or business) barriers. As an artist, you have direct control over only one of those: your interior creative life. At some point or another, thinking about your own art in terms of genre and definition—as "pop/rock" or "folk"—puts up as many walls for yourself as you would hope to break down. I try to make the music that makes me happiest, without regard to genre or reception. I think an important part of maturing as an independent artist is to understand what you can change and what you can't, what is your responsibility and what isn't. It is your responsibility to make the music you feel strongest about; it isn't your responsibility to label or define it. This is not to say there isn't a reason people talk about "folk" or "rock/pop"—you have to have some way of talking about music. But I like to keep that separate from the impulse to create music.

I also believe that audiences are way smarter than they are given credit for by the people who create the mechanical barriers between genres of music. People like good music, no matter if it's played on an acoustic guitar or comes from a bin labeled "rock." I see the answer as, "I didn't put the barrier there, neither did this audience, so together we are going to ignore it." You have to acknowledge these barriers (get your record in as many bins as possible!), but at the end of the day you have to continue your creative life without regard to them.

—Erin McKeown

❖ **Find a creative refuge.** Any artistic endeavor feels different once it is also (in full or in part) your livelihood. Everyone needs to preserve that feeling of creating just for the sake of creating, which is the wellspring of all great art. So make sure you get together with pals for jam sessions that have no professional purpose. Write an embarrassingly silly song that you'd never play in public. And, perhaps, cultivate an artistic interest outside of music.

I'm painting and drawing a lot, writing stories. I don't know, it all seems to feed each other and balance each other. Music and songs and touring and records—I love it; I can't imagine a better job in the world, but at the same time, it's a job and sometimes it feels like one when you are driving 500 miles a day and stopping at the radio station and going to the record store and doing the gig. So it's nice to have these other things that nobody knows much about. I really don't have to think about what anybody thinks about it. It's refreshing. It's like when I was 15 writing songs—it feels like that.

—Dan Bern

❖ ***Think, then act.*** As you navigate through the business, it's laudable to be independent-minded and suspicious of surrendering too much control of your music. But don't let that independent streak keep you from ever signing your name on the dotted line. Entering a business deal doesn't have to mean that you're selling out. You can preserve the integrity of what is most important—your songs—while working with other people to broaden the audience for what you do.

It's always possible (or even likely) that a relationship with a label or manager or agent won't deliver everything that you hoped for, but one of the ways you learn is by doing. Trust your gut instincts, keep your eyes open, and be especially careful when it comes to long-term agreements that you might regret in perpetuity. But when it looks and feels right, go for it. If you forever sit in your bedroom and grouse about how corrupt the music business is, your songs will never have the chance to get out in the world and make friends.

All business is not bad. A lot of people, and rightly so, go into the music business thinking they're going to get screwed. That's a healthy attitude to have, because then you're skeptical about anything that anybody puts in front of you, and that's what you should be. You should realize, though, that it's a sliding scale: skepticism does not necessarily equate into refusal to do a deal every time. Find out if it's a good business deal, and if it is, go for it, and hopefully you two are happy, you and the company you signed with.

—Kyle Staggs

❖ **Get real (but not too real).** Having a business partner not only gives you fewer balls to juggle all the time, but it shields you from some of the day-to-day frustrations of this line of work. In every music career there's a long line of unreturned calls, rejections, and dealings with people who are insensitive, indifferent, and abrasive. This isn't personal, but it feels like it is when your songs are on the line. So having someone else out there in the trenches on your

Dan Bern

behalf can help keep your spirits up and your eyes on the prize of making the best music you can.

> *For every song that my publisher gets cut, I'm going to go out on a limb and say that there are probably 100 or 150 songs she has played for somebody to get that one. Well, first of all, I don't want to deal with all that rejection of my own songs, day after day after day. She doesn't call me and say, "Hey, I played 30 of your songs for people today, and they passed on all of them." She just calls me about the one that they took. I guess what I'm trying to say is that we need to protect ourselves a little bit as creative souls, because our emotional state is wrapped up in some of this. I think it's healthy to know what's going on in the business, but if you become consumed by it, it's bound to affect your creative process in a negative way.*
>
> —Steve Seskin

❖ ***Give yourself credit.*** In all areas of life, we progress by setting our sights on the things we haven't done, the places we haven't been, the sounds we haven't created yet. Keep your eye on that horizon, but pause from time to time to consider the steps that you have taken: the songs written, the emotions shared, the music played. It takes a lot of nerve to get up in front of people, play something that you wrote, and invite them to respond. And if your song actually moves some people or makes them laugh or sets their feet dancing, that is an extraordinary accomplishment. In the face of all the steep odds, intense competition, and slim rewards of doing this instead of or in addition to what's affectionately known as a real job, sometimes you need to acknowledge how far you have come.

> *When people ask me about being an independent musician, I say, "Well, do you really have to do this? Do you have no alternative? Does this fuel your most inner soul? Will you die without getting your music out there? In that case, you have to do whatever it takes."*

It's a constant search. How do you establish an identity in the marketplace? How do you sustain a certain level of respect? "Oh, Jonatha's in town"—How do you establish that level of notoriety and persona? Sometimes you sit there and you think, "What the hell am I doing? I am this whiny creative mess and I suck and I'm never going to write another song and how are we going to pay the credit card this month ..." And then you kind of realize, "Wait a minute, I have been doing something. I have been working. I've been making small strides in a good direction."

—Jonatha Brooke

Small strides in a good direction: that sounds like a excellent motto. Small strides in a good direction, song to song to song. Happy travels.

RESOURCES

Here's a selective list of Web sites, publications, organizations, and other resources for further investigation of the subjects raised in this book. This entire text can be found on the Singer-Songwriter Resources page at www.jeffreypepperrodgers.com, where Web links are included wherever possible and the listings are regularly updated and expanded. At that page you will also find links to the author's books and articles that are of special interest to singer-songwriters.

WRITING

Music Instruction/Reference
Ben Bolt, *Music Theory for the Rock Guitarist,* Mel Bay.
Elvo S. D'Amante, *All About Chords,* Encore Music. In-depth study of chord theory and progressions, with exercises and quizzes.
Pat Pattison, *Writing Better Lyrics,* Writer's Digest Books.
Jack Perricone, *Melody in Songwriting: Tools and Techniques for Writing Hit Songs,* Hal Leonard.
Jeffrey Pepper Rodgers, ed., *Songwriting and the Guitar,* String Letter. Includes workshops on melody and lyric writing, chord theory and progressions, and guitar gear.
Rikky Rooksby, *How to Write Songs on the Guitar,* Backbeat Books. Detailed theory-based instruction on melody, harmony, rhythm, and chord progressions.
WholeNote, www.wholenote.com. Guitar site includes free lessons; see Basics section for guitar-oriented tutorials on music theory.
Guitar.to Player, www.guitar.to. Clever on-line programs for finding/ naming chords on piano and guitar (in standard tuning or any alternate tuning).
The Online Guitar Archive, www.olga.net. On-line guitar tablature.

Literary Guides
Annie Dillard, *The Writing Life,* Harper Perennial. An intense and poetic exploration of the creative process.

Anne Lamott, *Bird by Bird: Some Instructions on Writing and Life,*
  Anchor. A funny, smart, and encouraging book by a novelist and
  nonfiction writer.
William Strunk Jr. and E. B. White, *The Elements of Style,* Allyn and
  Bacon. The classic guide to clear and concise writing.

Software

Lyricist, Virtual Studio Systems, www.virtualstudiosystems.com.
  Versatile program for organizing and storing songs. Includes guitar
  chord diagrams, thesaurus, and rhyming dictionary.
SongMaster, Shubb, www.shubb.com. Software for building a database
  of songs (lyrics and chord charts), with tools for transposing and
  assembling set lists. Available with GigMaster (see Performing section) or by itself.

PERFORMING

Venues

Musi-Cal (www.musi-cal.com) and Mojam (www.mojam.com). Two entry
  points to the same huge database of live music events: use them to find
  venue ideas (including house concerts and off-the-beaten-track venues)
  and submit your own gigs for listing. Data is also licensed to other sites.
Pollstar, www.pollstar.com. Concert industry site includes a searchable
  database of events.
Houseconcerts.com. Site run by Texas house concert presenters lists
  venues and sells a book on hosting house concerts.
House Concerts, www.houseconcerts.org. Free, comprehensive guide
  to playing and hosting house concerts.
Folk venue listserv, lists.psu.edu/archives/folkvenu.html. Discussion list
  for presenters.
Acoustic Guitar Summer Study, www.acousticguitar.com. Listings of
  music camps and workshops, updated annually.
The *Dirty Linen* Gig Guide, www.dirtylinen.com. Concert listings.

Business

GigMaster, Shubb, www.shubb.com. Booking and tracking software for performers. Includes SongMaster (see Writing section above).

Jeri Goldstein, *How to Be Your Own Booking Agent and Save Thousands of Dollars,* New Music Times.

PowerGig, www.powergig.com. Resources/FAQ section includes sample performance contracts.

Quint Randle and Bill Evans, *Making Money Making Music: The Musician's Guide to Cover Gigs,* Backbeat Books. Focuses on starting a cover band but includes lots of nuts-and-bolts info and advice on gigging.

Alan Rowoth, www.alanrowoth.com. Tutorials page includes articles on booking, low-budget touring, and contracts.

Stage Craft and Gear

Dan Erlewine, *Guitar Player Repair Guide: How to Set Up, Maintain, and Repair Electrics and Acoustics,* Backbeat Books.

Frets.com. Exhaustive, illustrated on-line guide to acoustic guitar care and repair.

Steve Rapson, *The Art of the Solo Performer,* American Success Institute. The Web site affiliated with this book, www.soloperformer.com, offers tutorials on songwriting, touring, and the music business.

Jeffrey Pepper Rodgers, ed., *Performing Acoustic Music,* String Letter. Guide to stage craft includes an extensive section on choosing and using acoustic instruments.

Mike Sokol, *The Acoustic Musician's Guide to Sound Reinforcement and Live Recording,* Prentice Hall.

Simone Solondz, ed., *Acoustic Guitar Owner's Manual,* String Letter. Player's guide to guitar maintenance, with sections on traveling with and insuring your instrument.

RECORDING

Recording Process

Loren Alldrin, *The Home Studio Guide to Microphones,* Mix Bookshelf.

Jon Chappell, ed., *Digital Home Recording: Tips, Techniques, and Tools for Home Studio Production,* Backbeat Books.

David Franz, *Producing in the Home Studio with Pro Tools,* Berklee Press.

Mitch Gallagher, ed., *Make Music Now: Putting Your Studio Together, Recording Songs, Burning CDs, and Distributing Online*, Backbeat Books.

Ben Milstead, *Home Recording Power!* Muska and Lipman.

Huw Price, *Recording Guitar and Bass*, Backbeat Books.

Business

Bug Music, www.bugmusic.com. See FAQ for music publishing basics.

CD Baby, www.cdbaby.net. The "musicians' backdoor" of the indie music store has useful links and articles.

Folkweb, www.folkweb.com. Web store for indie folk and acoustic music.

Insound, www.insound.com. Rock-oriented indie music store.

The Music Biz Academy, www.musicbizacademy.com. Includes articles on promotion, copyright, and other business topics.

Oasis CD Manufacturing, www.oasiscd.com. Site includes "The Musicians' Guide to Replication, Mastering, and Promotion."

Diane Sward Rapaport, *How to Make and Sell Your Own Recording*, Prentice Hall.

Star Polish, www.starpolish.com. Extensive advice section covers all aspects of the record business.

United States Copyright Office, www.copyright.gov. Includes copyright basics, FAQ, and forms.

GENERAL BUSINESS

Judith Folkman, ed., *The Musicians' Atlas 2003*, Music Resource Group. Annual music-business directory.

Greg Forest, *The Complete Music Business Office*, Hal Leonard. More than 125 contracts and forms, on paper and on CD. Sample contracts can be found at bandradio.com/law/samples.html.

Bill Henderson, ed., *Pushcart's Complete Rotten Reviews and Rejections*, W.W. Norton. Comic relief for when you've heard too many discouraging words.

Michael Levine, *Guerrilla P. R.: How You Can Wage an Effective*

Publicity Campaign . . . Without Going Broke, HarperBusiness. Not written specifically about music, but applicable.

Donald S. Passman, *All You Need to Know About the Music Business,* Simon and Schuster. An authoritative, accessible, and highly readable guide.

Peter Spellman, *The Self-Promoting Musician: Strategies for Independent Music Success,* Berklee Press.

David Wimble, *The Indie Bible,* Big Meteor. Directory of radio stations, publications, sites for promoting music.

ORGANIZATIONS

Trade

Association for Independent Music, Courtney Proffitt, 925 W. Baseline Road #105-G, Tempe, AZ 85283; (480) 831-2954; www.afim.org.

Folk Alliance, 962 Wayne Ave., Suite 902, Silver Spring, MD 20910-4480; (301) 588-8185; www.folk.org.

Future of Music Coalition, c/o Michael Bracy, 1615 L Street NW, Suite 520, Washington, DC 20036; (202) 429-8855; www.futureofmusic.org. Focuses on technology and public policy.

Nashville Entertainment Association, P.O. Box 158029, Nashville, TN 37215; (800) 555-1212; www.nea.net. Membership services for breaking into the Nashville music industry.

Nashville Songwriters Association International, 1701 West End Ave., Third Floor, Nashville, TN 37203; (615) 256-3354; (800) 321-6008; www.nashvillesongwriters.com.

National Association for Campus Activities, 13 Harbison Way, Columbia, SC 29212; (803) 732-6222; www.naca.org. Connects educational institutions with entertainers.

The Songwriters Guild of America, 1500 Harbor Blvd., Weehawken, NJ 07086; (201) 867-7603; www.songwriters.org.

Performance Rights

ASCAP (New York), One Lincoln Plaza, New York, NY 10023; (212) 621-6000; www.ascap.com. On-line advice includes "Music and

Money: Where the Money Comes from for Writers and Publishers"
(www.ascap.com/musicbiz/money-intro.html).

BMI (New York), 320 West 57th Street, New York, NY 10019-3790;
(212) 586-2000; www.bmi.com. See "Songwriting and Copyright"
and "Music Publishing Terminology" (www.bmi.com/songwriter/
resources).

SESAC (headquarters), 55 Music Square East, Nashville, TN 37203;
(615) 320-0055; www.sesac.com.

SOCAN (headquarters), 41 Valleybrook Drive, Toronto, ON M3B
2S6, Canada; (416) 445-8700; (800) 55 SOCAN; www.socan.ca.
Canadian performing rights.

Mechanical Rights

Harry Fox Agency, 711 Third Ave., New York, NY 10017; (212) 370-
5330; www.harryfox.com. Central agency for mechanical licensing
in America—see Web site FAQ. Search for copyright and licensing
information on millions of published songs at www.songfile.com.

Canadian Musical Reproduction Rights Agency (CMRRA), 56
Wellesley St. W. #320, Toronto, Ontario M5S 2S3, Canada; (416)
926-1966; www.cmrra.ca.

Networking

Indiegrrl, www.indiegrrl.com. Networking for women in the independent music business.

Just Plain Folks, www.jpfolks.com. On-line community for people in
all aspects of the music business.

GENERAL RESOURCES

Web

The Muse's Muse, www.musesmuse.com. Vast clearinghouse of information, articles, and links for songwriters, including songwriting
contests and organizations.

Indie Music, www.indie-music.com. Advice and links for independent
musicians.

Harmony Central, www.harmony-central.com. Forums, lessons, gear info, and links for musicians.

Magazines

The Performing Songwriter, P.O. Box 4093, Nashville, TN 37204; (615) 385-7796; www.performingsongwriter.com.

Acoustic Guitar, P.O. Box 767, San Anselmo, CA 94979; (800) 827-6837; www.acousticguitar.com.

Sing Out! PO Box 5460, Bethlehem, PA 18015; (610) 865-5366; www.singout.org.

ACKNOWLEDGMENTS

Many of the artists' quotes in these pages come from interviews conducted for *Acoustic Guitar* magazine over a dozen years (some of which were collected in the book *Rock Troubadours*). I'm grateful to *Acoustic Guitar*'s publisher, David A. Lusterman, for permission to use published and unpublished excerpts from these conversations in this book. At the heart of *The Complete Singer-Songwriter* are the insights and advice generously offered over the years by so many musicians and sympathetic souls in the music business (yes, there are such people in the music business). So let me take a deep breath and thank: Rani Arbo, Dawn Atkinson, Dan Bern, Patrick Brayer, David Bromberg, Jonatha Brooke, Steve Brooks (Austin Conspiracy), Greg Brown, Malcolm Burn, Andrew Calhoun (Waterbug Records), Lauren Calista (Rounder Records), Beth Nielsen Chapman, Catie Curtis, Alana Davis, Ani DiFranco, Jerry Douglas, Stephen Fearing, Bob Feldman (Red House Records), Ferron, Holly Figueroa, Jim Fleming (Fleming and Associates), Nancy Fly and Seymour Guenther (Nancy Fly Agency), Jerry Garcia, Mike Gordon, David Grisman, Arlo Guthrie, Ben Harbert, Ben Harper, Richie Havens, Michael Hedges, Tish Hinojosa, Rob Hotchkiss, Chrissie Hynde, Jewel, Ken Irwin (Rounder Records), Lucy Kaplansky, Brandon Kessler (Messenger Records), Jennifer Kimball, Leo Kottke, Patty Larkin, Laura Love, Griff Luneberg (Cactus Café), Erin McKeown, Joni Mitchell, Skip Montanaro (Musi-Cal), Gurf Morlix, Peter Mulvey, Scott Nygaard, Tim O'Brien, Jim Olsen (Signature Sounds), Steven Page, Kelly Joe Phelps, Utah Phillips, Amy Ray, Harvey Reid, Tim Reynolds, Ed Robertson, Wayne Rooks (Serling, Rooks, and Ferrara), Emily Saliers, Dylan Schorer, Darrell Scott, Pete Seeger, Steve Seskin, Duncan Sheik, Paul Simon, Chris Smither, Jill Sobule, Simone Solondz, Kyle Staggs (Bug Music), Walkin' Jim Stoltz, Craig Street, James Taylor, Louise Taylor, Chris Thile, Jessica Baron Turner, Suzanne Vega, David Wilcox, and Chris Whitley.

Many thanks to David Hamburger, Paul Kotapish, and Teja Gerken for the valuable editorial feedback on my drafts; to Richard Johnston for the support and guidance in bringing this book into print; and to Stacey Lynn for the incisive editing. And especially to Cecilia, Lila, and Jasper for listening, caring, and singing along.

ABOUT THE AUTHOR

Jeffrey Pepper Rodgers has been pursuing his twin passions for words and music since he was a teenager. He became the founding editor of *Acoustic Guitar* magazine in 1990 and led the magazine through its tenth anniversary. These days he continues to write about all aspects of the music scene—and singer-songwriters in particular—for *Acoustic Guitar, Mojo,* and other publications, and he is a contributor to NPR's *All Things Considered.* Rodgers is the author of *Rock Troubadours: Conversations on the Art and Craft of Songwriting* (featuring Joni Mitchell, Paul Simon, James Taylor, Dave Matthews, Ani DiFranco, and others) and the *Beginning Guitarist's Handbook* (both from String Letter Publishing). He has also edited numerous books for musicians, including *Songwriting and the Guitar, Performing Acoustic Music,* and *The Acoustic Guitar Method.*

As a musician, Rodgers has been writing and playing original songs for 25 years. His home-recorded CD *Traveling Songs,* as well as his writings about music and other subjects, can be sampled at his web site, www.jeffreypepperrodgers.com.

Photo Credits

Jana Leon: page 2
Jay Blakesberg: pages 6, 12, 20, 70, 87, 105, 127
© Stephen Ide / Michael Ochs Archives.com: pages 17, 132
Ken Settle: pages 29, 42, 61, 83, 151, 161
© James Fraher / Michael Ochs Archives.com: page 58
Patrick Rock: page 99
Suzanne Mitchell: page 124
Michael Johnson: page 137
Petra Arnold: page 154
Patrick Rains: page 168
Pamela Murray: page 175
Jack Chester: page 179

INDEX

WHEN IT COMES TO MUSIC, WE WROTE THE BOOK.

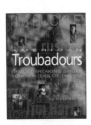
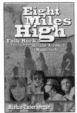